Plane Life

Highs and Lows

For Karen!
Life is a journey!
MBGolly

MARY BENNETT GOLLY

ISBN: 1501092316
ISBN 13: 9781501092312

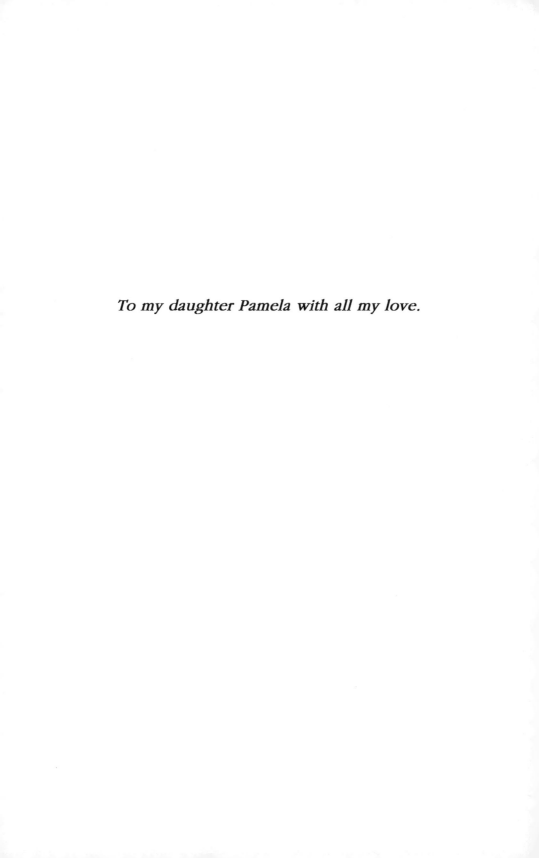

To my daughter Pamela with all my love.

Contents

Acknowledgements

I could not have dedicated so much of myself to this book without my husband John's relentless love and support.

I would like to thank Duane Smotherman, Lou Dozier and Barbara Fagan for showing me what it takes to ignite the fire back into my life, and teaching me the discipline that it takes to make a declaration and follow through with it.

I am grateful of my writers' critique group: first, Lorraine Haataia who invited me to join. Steve Brown who warned me I might cry if the critiquing got too personal. I thank Joan North for hosting us and for her uncanny ability in showing me how to 'cut to the chase'. Jodi Sykes' inspirational impetus and laughter, and Kathy Hynes, the comma queen. Brian Shea, thanks for great chapter re-titling and Ken Overman, for helping me sort out the 'streams of consciousness'. And lest I forget our snowbirds, Lori Thatcher and Joyce Nicholas who always brought fresh new insights.

A heartfelt thanks to my friends Arlene and Bill Thomsen, whose detailed editing added much needed polish to the manuscript.

Foreword

When is the exact moment that we know who we want to be? People often ask of children, "What would you like to be when you grow up?" Some say, "a doctor" or "a teacher." Many shrug their shoulders, and others say, "I don't know." And still some go on to college unsure of their choice in curriculum or major and settle for jobs they're not excited about doing.

In 1959, I took a trip from Japan to Greece on a TWA constellation airliner. It took two days to complete that journey. But something magical happened. I got the calling to become a stewardess when one of them befriended me during the flight.

There was family tension when I refuted my parents' wishes to go to finishing school in England. Instead, being the free spirit that I was, I flew from Europe to Miami to marry my first love whom I'd met during a vacation in Portugal.

Getting the job of my dreams wasn't easy. The first problem was my inability to conduct myself with confidence in large cattle call interviews. And then there were life's everyday obstacles.

But intention is a powerful force.

It wasn't until becoming a mother in my early thirties that I couldn't resist one last chance to apply for my dream job. There was no longer a retirement age for the career I'd so coveted. I finally actualized what I'd always wanted, but now there was a balancing act, more obstacles and seemingly endless tension. Could I continue working as a single mother and flight attendant? Choices had to be made. Some were easy. Others were difficult.

Airline bankruptcies made for troubled times as I struggled to keep my dream alive.

I had doubts, but also convictions. Self-examination led to awakenings: discarding and reinforcing beliefs. There were feelings of guilt from being away from home and wondering whether the job was enough to sustain happiness. And so my story begins.

One

Beginnings

She cussed him out passionately in Greek. Ronnie was apologetic yet smitten, but also frustrated that he couldn't communicate with her, except through body language. She couldn't speak English; he did not speak Greek. As she waved her arms at him with her reprimands, he kept apologizing and then just stood and stared at her. They finally realized they both could speak French, and fell in love.

It began as a World War II love story. My parents, Rose and Ronnie, met in 1945 in that bomb shelter which also served as a kitchen in the basement of the landmark Grand Bretagne Hotel in Athens. It had been converted into a refuge for dignitaries and their families.

Rose was the stepdaughter of Angelos Evert, the chief of police in Athens, a man who was a philanthropist, saving many Jewish people's lives by issuing them alias identification credentials. His family had immigrated to Greece from Bavaria in the 1800's. His wife's name was Mary.

My father Ronnie, a British army captain, was on assignment in Greece and residing at the same hotel. Prior to being dispatched to Athens, he had fought in the Desert War in North Africa, the turning point for the allied forces and a victory for the free world. A British expatriate, he grew up in Sao Paolo, Brazil, where the Bennett family owned tobacco plantations. In 1942 Ronnie went to college in England before volunteering into the army.

As he walked through swinging doors in the basement-kitchen that fateful day, they bumped into each other, spilling tea all over the one dress that Rose had with her. Her trip to the Grande Bretagne happened in the middle of the night just a couple of months prior.

When Ronnie proposed to Rose she was only sixteen years old. Her parents were reluctant to let her go at such a young age, but they loved Ronnie. My mother later told me that she'd listen to them argue behind closed doors about whether or not to let her marry at such a young age. She was madly in love and hoped that they would.

They were married within a few months, in September of 1945.

With the World War ended, they moved to Sao Paolo, Brazil—nearly half the world away from Rose's home and family. I was born seven years later, in 1952. My father worked for Goodyear, starting as an accountant, and eventually becoming a finance director.

We left Brazil two years after my birth. And so the wanderlust seeds were planted.

This was the beginning of my world travels. We moved to Cuba for a short while, but Battista's government was about to be overthrown by the Communist regime led by Fidel Castro. My parents found an empty coffin at their front door and took that as a sign to flee. I don't recall much about Cuba except that my mom raved about it years later. She often spoke about the wonderful food, their music, and dance clubs.

My father's assignments with the tire company took us from Cuba to Puerto Rico, where my sister Pam was born, becoming the first U.S. citizen by birth in our family.

We got to live in Japan a couple of years later. I didn't like Japanese food. Everything seemed like it had to be eaten raw. But our maids also knew how to prepare Western dishes too, so that's what we ate regularly in addition to my mother's Mediterranean cooking.

I remember perfectly manicured and colorful Japanese gardens. We'd visit a park that had large koi fishponds. The fish were so pretty in their bright orange and white. We fed them bread for many hours. They'd scramble for each morsel with mouths wide open, their vivid fins splashing about the surface of the water as they fought to catch the pieces of bread.

I have pictures of us wearing kimonos. Mom took lessons in flower arranging, so we always had beautiful flowers in vases around the house. Our housekeepers doted on us. The live-in maids became part of our family. I thought everyone lived that way, moving around to different places with maids and nannies, not realizing how unique a lifestyle we had. The maids did most of the housework and cooking, but I was taught to make my own bed and tidy up after myself. We had to learn Japanese—a difficult language that I can no longer speak. "You'll appreciate travelling and learning foreign language someday," said Papa—the term we used to say "Dad."

My first recollections began during those impressionable young years. I looked forward to flying every time we moved or went on vacation. Planes fascinated me. I was bitten by the travel bug, and always became excited with the sights and sounds of planes flying in the sky.

In 1959, Goodyear transferred us to Portugal. Since my mom was pregnant with my brother Chris, the move was too much for her to handle all at once. So plans were made to stop in Greece, where we'd live in Athens for two months awaiting my brother's birth. My dad continued on to Lisbon to begin his new assignment. We'd join him after Chris' birth. I was seven.

It took two days to make the trip to Athens from Tokyo—no jets then. We flew the state-of-the-art Lockheed Constellation, affectionately known as the "Super Connie," on Trans World Airlines. That plane had the shape of a slim dolphin. Painted in white, the logo and world insignia were outlined in red.

People dressed in their best attire to travel in the fifties and sixties. I wore a plaid skirt with a white blouse tucked in, a blue sweater, and white socks with patent leather shoes. My chestnut-brown hair was neatly combed and swept to one side with a clip. I felt special as I boarded the plane. The wind was blowing and I could smell jet fuel, a sour smell I would grow to like, known as Jet A fuel.

The stewardess greeted us warmly. She was impeccable, wearing a fitted uniform suit with a hat and white gloves. As beautiful as she was friendly, she wore a lot of makeup and bright red lipstick. I'd never seen anyone so glamorous and polished. When we were airborne, I watched every move she made. Noticing my eyes following her, she asked me if I wanted to help her serve peanuts while she served the drinks.

"Don't forget to smile and place the peanuts neatly next to the drink, on top of the paper napkin. And be sure that this *T.W.A.* logo on the peanut package faces them."

I did what I was told and felt so happy playing "stewardess." When I sat back down next to my mother, I announced, "When I grow up, I want to be a stewardess." She smiled, pleased at my enthusiasm.

There were sleeperettes on the plane —beds that folded out from beneath the luggage racks—but I was so excited that I don't remember sleeping much. I looked outside the window at night and saw the bright moon shining in the distance, and the strobe lights on the wings that flickered continuously. I tried counting them and fell asleep. Then morning came and I looked at the ground below me. The sky and land had a foggy grayish-blue hue. I noticed lights still on in the little houses below. It felt like we weren't moving at all. But the loud engines told me otherwise.

We made two stopovers, one in Bombay (present day Mumbai), India and the other in Cairo, Egypt. My mother said it was for refueling, but there also, different stewardesses came to replace the ones that got off. I wondered where they went. The lady who had enlisted my help earlier hugged me tightly before she left. I said goodbye to her tearfully. I've often wondered what became of her. When parting, I told her that when I grew up, I'd be a stewardess too.

"You're going to be a wonderful stewardess someday, my dear," she said.

Two

The Gypsy Life

We arrived in Athens, tired. Especially my mother as she was nearing the end of the pregnancy term, her tummy big and round. Flying as an expectant mother with two young children couldn't have been easy. Even at age seven I could see that. My little sister Pam clung to her, unwilling to be still unless she was on her lap. She'd scream when she didn't get her way. As a young toddler if she didn't get what she wanted it was pandemonium. I believe that her determination so early in life developed who she is today and was instrumental in her success as a small business owner.

Mom seemed at peace no matter how difficult the travels were and never complained. There was some normal sibling rivalry, but I was the eldest and was supposed to "know better" than to pick fights. I was supposed to behave like a young lady. Maybe some oldest-child pent up frustration led to my sense of independence later on.

My grandparents met us after the long two-day trip and took us to an apartment they'd found for us. It was just a block up the street from where they lived. That was our residence for three months or so, depending on when Chris decided to be born.

It was a time of family bonding getting to know my grandparents. I'd heard mom talk about her mother, saying how much she missed her and my grandfather, "Papou". Mom hadn't seen her parents since she married my dad in 1945 to live in Brazil. It made me sad that so much time had passed before this tearful reunion.

How could one live so far apart from one's Mommy and Daddy? I vowed that would never happen to me.

My Yaya was a loving grandmother who spent a lot of time with me. She had white hair. She wore a blue and white seersucker robe with lace trim most of the time. She felt so soft when we hugged, and I loved sitting close to her, cuddling whenever I could. We'd sit on the sofa and she'd read to me, or teach me how to draw. She drew faces in pencil and I liked drawing flowers. She'd spend hours showing me how to manipulate a pencil on paper, drawing lines and shadows, faces and flowers, trees and landscapes—tiny thumbnail renditions that looked so perfect. She was talented and I wanted to emulate her art, even though it was just doodling. In later years, art became one of my favorite hobbies. I attributed her influence on me at a solo art exhibit many years later.

Strangers came to the door sometimes. They wanted to talk to my grandfather. He'd welcome them in his study and spend hours with them before saying goodbye as they'd leave with tears and what seemed like immense appreciation. I later found out these were Greek Jews whose relatives had been spared with my grandfather's help during the Nazi occupation. They were paying homage to express gratitude.

I wondered if my grandparents ever travelled like we did.

"Have you ever been on an airplane before, Yaya?" I asked.

"No, dear, never."

Oh I thought everyone did.

"Well it's so much fun. When you fly and look out the window, the houses and cars look small, like toys. And there are stewardesses on the plane to serve you drinks and food."

"That's very nice," Yaya said. She didn't seem to share my enthusiasm.

"You could take a plane to come and visit us."

"I will, someday," She promised.

"I'm going to be a stewardess when I grow up," I told her.

Chris was born a few weeks after we arrived. There was a big fanfare—it was a boy—the Bennett name would be carried on, my mother told us. How silly. My name is Bennett too. Why did I have to be a boy to carry that name?

"Girls get married and take their husband's last name." Mom said when I asked her.

"But why can't a husband take his wife's name?" I asked. After some explaining, I understood the meaning of tradition.

My sister Pam didn't appreciate our brother's arrival. She had been the baby of the family for two years, and he took up too much of her time on mom's lap. But like most siblings, she adapted.

We didn't have electronic games that overtook households in the nineteen-eighties. Our amusement consisted of dolls, train sets, coloring books and Lego blocks. And imagination. I loved to read as soon as I was old enough, and was read to often at bedtime before then. I spent many hours leafing through the National Geographic magazine collection at my grandparents' house. The pictures were breathtakingly amazing—places I'd never seen and vivid close-ups of scary animals like tigers and snakes. I learned about aborigines, and various other cultures. I felt mesmerized as I took in each picture as if it was a new window into the world. They had the Encyclopedia Britannica. I spent hours looking through the pages of knowledge that felt overwhelming at times.

My favorite game was pretending I was a stewardess on a flight. I'd line up dining room chairs two by two in an airplane configuration with an aisle in between the pairs, and then serve my imaginary passengers food and drink. I had imaginary passengers, but my sister would play along as a passenger too when she felt like it.

Chris' arrival meant that we'd soon be joining my dad in Lisbon. I missed him and looked forward to being together as a family again. And of course there would be another plane ride. I wondered what our new house would look like. I couldn't wait for the big freight truck that would arrive with our furniture and belongings—my own bed.

Saying goodbye to my grandparents was painful, and we all cried. Worse, and even more heartbreaking was to witness my mother sobbing. We clung to each other not wanting to let go, hugging and kissing each other over and over. I already missed my Yaya since I didn't know when we'd see her again.

"We live the gypsy life!" my Mom often said with a touch of humor.

It was a way of life I became accustomed to. Except that it meant leaving people whom I'd grown fond of or loved deeply and thought I might never see again. My favorite school teachers. Friends.

"You'll have a nice new school with good teachers, and make new friends," Mom said. While I knew that, it didn't make the transition easier, and I felt melancholy each time. I was shy and clung to my mom a lot. The first day of school wherever we lived was painful. The other students were overly curious about me and I felt like an outsider.

"You'll be thankful someday, Sheika, very few people get to travel like you," my Papa once told me. Sheika was the nickname they'd given me as a baby in Brazil, which stuck. Family and close friends call me Sheika to this day, even though I was named Mary Angela after my Yaya Mary and Papou Angelos.

We went to Greece each summer to visit our Greek family. We looked forward to this annual trip. Summers were hot, and we spent many days on the beaches. I loved the smell of wild eucalyptus and rosemary and the crystal clear seawater. We ate well at outdoor taverns and I came to savor Greek food. It tasted like no other, fresh and flavorful.

"It's your heritage," Mom would say.

But I always looked forward to the next flight, no matter where it was headed. Wanderlust had set in. It felt like an adventure.

But one day I discovered that flying didn't exactly agree with me. I became air sick, which was emotionally upsetting. Why was this happening to me?

On one flight from Athens to Lisbon, when it was time to deplane, I stood up and walked forward to exit, and threw up all over the beautiful and impeccably dressed stewardesses who were bidding us farewell.

"Oh, don't worry—you poor little girl, let me get you a warm towel to wash up," one of them said, patiently. They were so nice and I was so embarrassed. Their kindness impressed me. How could I make such a mess! They're so nice to me and I made a mess!

My dad suggested I take Dramamine for airsickness from then on.

But on the next trip when we were headed to live in Paris for Papa's next assignment, I'd forgotten to bring the Dramamine with me. It was packed in our luggage.

"I'm not sitting next to her," my sister Pam yelled in the aisle as we boarded, starting up a temper tantrum.

"Me neither. She'll vomit all over us," Chris said.

"You'll never be a stewardess! You throw up all the time!" Pam said.

I never forgot to take my medicine again after that episode. I threw up multiple times. Trying to contain myself made matters worse. My stomach heaved dry sour saliva and fluids. I thought I'd die. My siblings were no help either with their loud exclamations of "eeeeuw!"

When I flew the next time, I was fully medicated and slept for that entire flight. When I woke up to deplane, I was dizzy with sleep. That made me sad because I wanted to enjoy every minute of the flight, from takeoff, lunch time, and landing. But at least I didn't throw up...

Would I ever outgrow this?

The next residence was Paris. I suffered when my siblings and I were put into a French school to immerse us into the language and culture, and get "a better education" as Papa put it. The problem was, I couldn't say a word in French except for 'bonjour' and 'oui'. Nor could I understand people speaking to me. It was my first experience in bullying. I was jeered at, kids pointing their finger at me mockingly. I was left out of their games during recess. At age nine I felt very lonely. I wanted to run away. I'd go home crying, begging my parents to take me out of that school.

"But you must learn to speak French," my father said. They got me a tutor and I caught up very quickly. Soon, I was learning grammar and math in French, and became fluent in the language.

We moved to Rome a few years later. I continued going to a French school except that it was a catholic school this time. I loved that school. There was structure and peace there and the nuns were all very nice. I took classes in Italian and learned yet another language—Greek while listening to my mother talk on the phone to her parents. We'd visit Athens every summer for vacation where I got to practice what I'd learned and add even more new words to my vocabulary.

"Someday you'll appreciate knowing all these languages," Papa said repeatedly.

Latin, the dead language, was a required course. I couldn't figure out why and the only explanation I could think of was it was for brain exercise.

It did help my brain get wired to learn foreign languages while we spoke English at home.

I disliked math. But I loved art, and literature.

Our stay in Rome lasted three years. Although I went to the protected enclave of a the Catholic school, I was given plenty of freedom to roam around.

At the age of thirteen I took buses and went around town and met friends from school at the Piazza di Spagna. I'd get an ice cream gelato there each time. We'd get together at each others' houses and listen to Beatles music.

The name of my school was the Institut Saint Dominique where I became more and more fond of the nuns, my teachers. Was it their servitude that paralleled stewardesses, albeit not in such a glamorous way? I shared my feeling with Papa freely.

"I love the nuns. I want to become one when I grow up," I told him.

That's when he decided it was time to remove me from the Catholic school.

"No daughter of mine will become a nun," Papa said. It was just in time when he received his new assignment and another move for us.

Back to Lisbon. I was fifteen. We had our usual stay at a five star hotel while my parents went house hunting. Goodyear gave us a generous amount of time—three months to accomplish this.

At our temporary hotel arrangement, the Hotel Palacio in Estoril, I met and fell in love with a boy named Mike. He was the son of a Czechoslovakian father and Austrian mother who'd become U.S. citizens. His father worked for the United States State Department. We later figured out he was in the C.I.A. Mike called his father a "spook" which was slang for spy. They were in Portugal for a summer vacation.

Although I was only fifteen, my parents liked Mike and his family well enough to let us go out for a few hours in the evenings. We'd go to local discotheques. The first kiss sent me swooning and I thought that this was the kind of love that meant forever. Marriage. I couldn't think of ever loving anyone else.

Sadly their vacation came to an end and we moved into a house my parents found. We resumed normal routine of school and family life. But the stay in Portugal was short lived. We'd barely lived in the new the house when Papa came home with a new announcement about another assignment.

Goodyear was opening a plant in Thessaloniki, Greece. The new executive offices would be located in Athens. Papa was invited to break ground there for Goodyear and to be the first executive to inaugurate this new venture. My mother shouted with joy. We kids picked up on that and did a happy dance of sorts around the living room.

The Bennett family was finally going to Athens to live. Although we knew the gypsy life was far from over, I felt like our family had come full circle with all the moves.

The entire family flew First Class this time, I suppose because my father had reached a certain level as an executive. I made sure I took my airsickness pill and worked hard at staying awake. It was my first experience of caviar and champagne served by a gracious stewardess on Olympic Airways 707 jet bound for Athens.

Three

A TEENAGER IN ATHENS

*O*ur temporary hotel residence was the Grande Bretagne, where my parents met and fell in love so many years earlier. When they found a permanent place to live, the next decision was where to send us to school.

Please—no Greek school. They have a weird alphabet…Will I go to a French school again?

They settled on the American Academy. The school was highly recommended and graduating kids went on to big name colleges like Duke and Harvard. I hadn't thought about college yet.

I entered the American Academy as a Freshman. The curriculum was easy compared to the European education system where homework used to keep me up late at night. I kept my French studies current by taking the advanced classes. I joined the school's art and language clubs My art teacher, Mr. Piladakis, was very influential and took a liking to me—paying special attention to my work and said that I had artistic talent. He spent extra time teaching me new painting techniques. We had a student exhibit in town where I sold one of my first paintings to a TWA executive's wife. It was a paper mache overlay of the Aegean with faded mountains at the horizon. I was proud of myself.

I made new friends again. Some were kids from the Air Force, diplomatic corps and corporate-sector families, mostly U.S. expatriates. One of my best friends was a girl named Alda. She was a couple of years younger than I but we were neighbors and shared many walks together to each others' homes. We chatted and listened to Beatles' music. Her mom, Athena, always had the best snacks for us after school, so I'd get off at Alda's bus stop because I loved the American goodies they'd get from the PX. My favorite was 'Moon Pies'.

The mid sixties culture of the hippie era that had been borne in the United States filtered into the school's student body. It was cool to dress like hippies. I was fascinated by their lifestyle and was curious enough to try smoking hashish and dressing like Cher, which was hobo style with glam and not sloppy-dirty like some others did. I don't think I would have enjoyed the Woodstock concert. It was a three-day outdoor event with great music but no bathing. My experience with smoking pot was a dabbling here and there. On the first toke, I'd cough and tears would fill my eyes. I felt like I'd choke to death. It tasted horrible but I got used to it. I hate to admit I did it more so to fit in than for the enjoyment of it, a need I was happy to outgrow in later years.

We had school dances, but no one asked me to dance. Although there was no language barrier, I was still different to most of the kids who came from the U.S. where I'd never been before. They spoke about their home states and I'd listen to their stories. I was shy and my parents didn't encourage my participating in co-ed activities much. There was talk of promiscuous behavior. I'd heard of girls "doing it" with boys and the thought disgusted me. So, no real boyfriends. I had male friends, but nothing serious. There were some cute boys that I would've liked to know better, but my heart was with Mike. I missed him and hoped we'd marry someday like we'd promised.

I saw my grandparents monthly and learned to speak Greek fluently, although reading it still posed a challenge. I spent many hours learning how to read the crazy words in the local newspapers. It was like deciphering code.

We had a beautiful penthouse apartment in Paleon Phaleron, close to Hellinkon Airport. Our large balcony was on the direct approach pattern for airliners. The jets brought a deafening noise to the area neighborhoods. Windows rattled and the floor shook. I loved that.

We overlooked the Aegean Sea, with the isle of Aegina in the background that separated sea and sky. Papa and I spent lots of time on that balcony playing chess or watching airplanes. That was where I learned to identify different aircraft types. We'd play guessing games when Papa would quiz me. We could see the aircraft numbers under the wings as they flew over our heads just before making it to the landing strip a few miles away. Jet fuel smells permeated the air. I wondered about the stewardesses aboard those flights and hoped that someday I'd be flying like them.

Mike and I corresponded by mail twice weekly. He told me he missed me and that we'd marry someday.

"Wait for me. I'll finish school and we'll be together," he'd write.

He was attending a school in Gstaad, Switzerland. His parents had bought him his first car, a black Jaguar XKE. He too experimented with hashish. We shared the same taste in music. The repertoire grew from The Beatles to the Rolling Stones and some more 'psychedelic' brands like Pink Floyd, Moody Blues, and Jimi Hendrix. My parents tolerated Beatles tunes being played loudly on my record player, but winced at the sounds of Jimi Hendrix's screeching guitar sounds. Artistic license had also given way to powerful anti-war messages.

Papa was somewhat amused by Country Joe and the Fish's song, with the lyrics that went: *"come on all big strong men-Uncle Sam needs your help again-got himself in a terrible jam-way down yonder in Viet Nam..."* A music lover himself, he shared my passion for the Moody Blues. We spent time listening to my records. In return, he shared his passion for classical music and I grew to love Tchaikovsky and Rimsky Korsakov. His deceased mother was a concert pianist at one time and music was part of the Bennett family.

One day I got a telegram from Mike.

"I'm in Israel working at a Kibbutz-stop-would like to pass by Athens on my way back home-stop-can I stay at your house?"

My heart skipped a beat. I asked Papa if he could come.

"How long is he going to stay?"

"I don't know. He's on his way back to Switzerland. Please, Papa?"

We picked Mike up a week later and he settled into our guest room. He shared stories about working at a Kibbutz. I showed him around Athens. We went to the Acropolis, Plaka and several museums, and talked incessantly about future plans.

"I want to be a stewardess when I graduate."

"That'll be great. We can't have children then—not for a while at least," he said.

We smoked hashish and hoped we wouldn't get caught. I couldn't imagine what the consequences might have been and didn't want to think about it. I sneaked into his bedroom one night. It was my first experience with sex and it was wonderful. *This is true love.*

I was sure of that.

The next morning I couldn't look my parents in the eye, although I still felt I'd done the right thing. After all, I was going to marry Mike someday. I ruminated and rationalized that I wasn't promiscuous like some of the girls I knew.

He left after a five days and I felt devastated and lonely, even with the promise of a future together. I ached in the pit of my stomach.

Mom tried setting me up on dates with sons of ship owner magnates.

"You can fall in love again, Sheika, you're too young not to date others. It's time now." she said.

"You married Papa and you were only sixteen, you didn't go out with anyone else. You knew…" I argued, to no avail.

The following weekend, a young man by the name of Alexandros took me out. He had a red Ferrari and scared me to death as he drove the coastal road, "Paraleea" to the restaurant, weaving through normal traffic. *Show off.*

We ate a lavish dinner. Fish, calamari accompanied by potatoes au gratin.

"Wine?" he asked.

"No I don't drink."

"Really? Well you should try some. It's good wine."

I took a sip and nothing more. The conversation was stifling.

"What are your future plans?"

"I'm going to be a stewardess."

"Oh that's not a good plan. Your mother said you're an artist. You should be an artist."

"I like to paint, but I want to become a stewardess and travel. I love to travel."

"You don't know what you really want. You're too young."

We went to a club where friends of his met us and there was music and dancing. But not the kind of music I was listening to. It was too—stuffy.

When I got home I told mom not to set me up on any more dates.

"He's a rich spoiled show off" I said.

"But there are others, their fathers are ship owners and the families have a lot of money."

"Is that all that matters?" I shouted. At seventeen I became rebellious. The era of hippies had this slogan that went *"Don't Trust Anyone Over Thirty."* I took that very seriously. My parents were well over that age as were most people with any kind of authority.

"No, darling. You don't have to marry to be well off. After you go to college or finishing school you'll have your own career. But it's good to have money."

I went out on a few other blind dates but was not impressed. One man was nice and sweet, but there was no spark for me, he wasn't good looking—too tall and very skinny.

Later I accepted a date from a cute high school boy. We went to a movie. He wanted sex right after dinner. I left him at the park bench and walked home alone.

My parents decided to divorce after twenty-five years of marriage. It broke my heart. There was upheaval during my teen years I could have done without. Fighting. What happened to happy times?

A letter came from Mike telling me he was going to Miami to work for a friend's company, National Airlines, as a ramp person. Ramp people handled baggage and fueled the planes.

"I'm not college bound. I didn't make very good grades," he wrote. I thought it would be a good job for him and for us to start our life. And when I'd be old enough—I had to be twenty-one—perhaps National Airlines would hire me as a stewardess. That seemed perfect.

Shortly before graduating from the American Academy, Papa announced, "We've made all the arrangements for you. Your cousin in London is very happy to have you live with her. You'll attend a finishing school there. You'll love living in London."

"But I can't!"

I tried convincing my parents that marrying Mike was a better choice.

"Finishing school will be better," Papa said.

Finishing school—what did *that* mean? Finishing what? I liked the word starting. Not finishing. It just made much more sense.

I went to bed crying that night. I looked forward to the milestone event of graduating from high school. I was up for awards in art and languages. The ceremony was held at an ancient amphitheater at the foot of the Acropolis. More than anything, this was going to be the end of school and beginning of independence.

And all I wanted to think about was flying. A job as a stewardess someday.

Four

A New World

"Please let me go!" I said.

"You're too young to get married," said Papa

"You'll be too far away," said Mom.

I rebelled and insisted on my parents letting me fly to Miami and marry Mike. It was all I could think about—obsessively so. A finishing school in England was not what I wanted. I never understood the concept of *finishing*. I wasn't interested in college. I later came to regret that and felt inferior to people who'd gotten their degrees. But I'd made up in my own mind, I was going to *starting* school. Not finishing. The start of a new life.

I finally convinced my parents that unless they'd allow me passage to the U.S. I'd elope. They let me go—reluctantly.

"I'm going to miss you so much," said Mom with tears in her eyes, which made me sad. I thought about the distance that once existed between her and her parents.

"We'll see each other. Especially when I become a stewardess and can fly anywhere I want," I rationalized. "I promise. And you'll get passes to fly and come see me."

I had to get a visa to live in the United States. My British passport wasn't enough. The process took weeks and there was a list of things I had to do. I had to get a chest x-ray to ensure I didn't have tuberculosis or any other contagious diseases. My inoculations had to be up to date. I had to take an oath at the U.S. Embassy swearing that I wasn't a communist or a prostitute. A marital visa was finally granted with the proviso that Mike and I would wed within three months after my arrival. I couldn't wait. My spirits soared with excitement.

I'm going to the United States!

But as brave and rebellious as I'd become, I was also afraid about going so far away. I promised I would write to my family and friends. Fear turned to excitement and anticipation.

We kissed and hugged and cried.

Am I running away? Will I be happy with Mike? Am I making the right decision?

*All children must get their wings and fly…like birds do…*I rationalized. Flip flops in my tummy and all.

I flew to Miami on a Pan Am jet. Afraid of being airsick, I took Dramamine. I watched the stewardesses and admired their sky blue uniforms with white short sleeve blouses. Their perfect hairdos and lipstick, and their smiles as they served everyone. I could really see myself doing this.

There was a stopover in San Juan, Puerto Rico, the U.S. port-of-entry customs and immigration clearance checkpoint. I was wearing a blue suede mini skirt with tights, a poet blouse with puffy long sleeves and tall black boots, and felt all grown up. I handed the immigration officers my paperwork. X-rays. British passport.

"So you're going to get married?" said a tall man with a gruff voice.

"Yes."

"Best of luck," he said, stamping my passport and keeping my x-rays.

Finally we landed at Miami International Airport. It was still light out. I had to get used to the seven-hour time change from Greece. I walked down the air stairs and into the airport and felt the warm humid breezes caressing my face, making my hair fly around. The Beatles had landed there once and I remembered the famous pictures of them walking down the Pan Am air stairs on every magazine cover.

I eagerly sought Mike in the crowd waiting along the fence and spotted him standing a few feet away among others awaiting friends and family. We embraced, and after retrieving my luggage, headed to the new apartment he'd found in South Miami, a short distance from the airport. He drove a 1968 VW Beetle.

"I love this car!" I said as we loaded it with my luggage and took off.

"Can you drive it?" he asked.

"Of course, but not right now." I was tired.

There were makes and models of cars on the road that I'd never seen before. Buicks, Chevrolets, Fords. They all looked so foreign. Cars in Europe were much smaller, and there were no expressways where I lived. Feeling intimidated, I wondered if I'd ever learn how to find my way around.

"It's going to be an adjustment," said Mike. "Everything is so different here—not like Europe. No public transportation—or very little at best. We have grocery stores where you can get everything you need in one place, instead of individual stores like bakeries and delis."

I was used to taking buses and trains to get anywhere. "You'll need to drive everywhere here," Mike said.

We went to our furnished apartment and I unpacked. I wasn't used to air-conditioning. It felt luxurious. I marveled at the wall-to-wall carpeting. We smoked a joint then ordered pizza. Awhile later some of his friends stopped by to meet me. I was tired but happy. They were curious to know about the places I'd lived.

"You have a funny accent," said Will, one of Mike's closest friends and co-workers at National. It wasn't a strong British accent, but I sounded foreign and not very American. It made me feel self-conscious.

The next morning I was eager to prove I'd be a wonderful wife who could cook and make home life pleasant. That was something Mom always exuded. I wanted to emulate her that way. Although we once had maids, she cooked a lot and taught me how to as well. I enjoyed those moments together.

"It's something every woman should learn," she'd tell me.

I made a grocery list when Mike left for work. Feta cheese. Olive oil. Onions. Tomatoes. Pasta. Greek olives. A loaf of bread. Mint leaves for Greek meatballs. Grand Union, the grocery store was right next door so I walked since Mike had taken the car to work.

That was the day that I realized I had indeed come into a different world, and went through a "culture shock".

The grocery store had no loaves of bread like I was used to. They only had one kind: sliced white Wonder Bread. *Ugh*. I walked up and down every isle in the store looking for Greek olives, finding only canned green olives with red peppers in them. When I asked the store clerks where I could find olive oil, they looked at me, puzzled.

"Hon, the only oil we have is vegetable oil, or Crisco if you're fryin'."

Feta cheese was unheard of.

I bought spaghetti and a can of tomato sauce, some lettuce, tomatoes and onions. This would have to do.

"Those are things we might be able to find in some specialty store," Mike said after I lamented not finding what I'd been looking for.

As time passed newer grocery stores opened and imports became staples on the shelves. Many people hadn't even heard about the foods I was accustomed to unless they went to ethnic restaurants—or travelled to Europe.

I called my Mom, having to go through an operator first. It was the only way to make a long distance call in the early 1970's. I missed her terribly even though I was content with my decision.

"Mom, can you believe we don't have Feta? Or mint leaves?"

"I'll bring you some one day," she said. "I miss you. Are you happy?"

Even if I weren't, I wouldn't tell her. I'd come too far to even think that way. I'd be embarrassed to say I wanted to come back home. It was a struggle but we managed.

Mike had his job and I began looking for one as well—a temporary one until I'd be twenty-one and could become a stewardess, the minimum hiring age. I had three years to wait, and then I could fly for about fourteen before settling down and having children. There was a cut-off age—typically thirty-five years old for stewardesses at that time. But a career that would last a little over a decade seemed good to me. I couldn't wait.

We married a month later at the justice of the peace. Although I'd envisioned a different sort of wedding day when I was a little girl, I felt very grown up as a new Mrs. We wore hippie clothes, jeans and white blouse, my hair was parted in the middle and long past my shoulders. Will's wife, Rosemarie got flowers to put in my hair and made me a small bouquet. They were our witnesses.

My parents and I corresponded by mail regularly, and on the phone once in awhile. We couldn't afford many long distance calls. It was too expensive.

And the connection was so bad we practically had to shout on the phone to be heard. I wrote about Miami and what I was doing, and they shared their news with me.

It broke my mother's heart that I forgot to tell her we'd gotten married right away. I remembered it only after sealing the envelope, and wrote a one-line sentence on the back to say "by the way, Mike and I got married last week."

What was I thinking?

This created a rift between us. She called me crying to ask why we hadn't planned something nicer that the family could attend. I had no answer and struggled with guilt for years after that.

A year later our parents provided a nice down payment for our first house. I later found out that Mike had become used to getting large sums of money from them and it annoyed me. My father had always taught us to live within our means, even though I wasn't yet sure what that meant. We were two spoiled kids being lavished and unable to learn the true meaning of independence and self-sufficiency. We partied a lot after work and life seemed too easy. But our parents weaned us off the easy life and we started learning what it took to make a living.

I found a job at a warehouse for a women's clothing chain store called Size 5-7-9 shops. I worked alongside a fun-loving black girl who trained me on receiving shipments and tagging clothing to send to the stores at the malls. I was told to never discuss pay.

We were both due for a raise a few months later. After receiving our checks, we chatted excitedly about getting the extra pay and how we were going to celebrate.

"How much do you make?"

"$2.80 an hour," I said. I knew immediately that I'd slipped. Her eyes turned big and round and she became silent.

"What do you make?" I asked.

"$2.00," She said. "It's not fair. I've been here longer than you and I work just as hard." I couldn't believe it and I felt so sorry. She'd been my mentor and trainer.

She immediately headed to the boss' office. We were both fired on the spot. I'd read about slavery and emancipation in America but I couldn't believe that prejudices still existed in 1972. I felt terrible for it. How could anyone look down upon another because of one's background or color?

I got a job as a clerk in the Dade County Courthouse. I was happy to work again but was bored typing and filing and sitting at a desk all day for five days a week. I couldn't wait until I was twenty-one and could apply for my dream job. I wanted to wear that pretty uniform, fly and visit new places.

Five

FAILURES AND LESSONS

I thought it would be easier. Few airlines were hiring in 1973. There was a fuel crisis and the air carriers began to cut their schedules. I put out applications nonetheless. Someone told me that they kept those on file until they'd start hiring again. Thankfully being married was allowed, but I still worried about a date I'd have to quit. Some airlines allowed stewardesses to fly until age thirty-five, but that was tops.

The first carrier I got an interview with was National Airlines. They were a small airline with a logo of the sun on the tail of their planes. They had catchy TV advertisements featuring flirty stewardesses saying "Hi, I'm Betsy, come fly me." In today's world that would be considered sexist, but back then it was the image—sexy and well groomed, the look that travelling executives enjoyed.

I put my long brown hair up in an elegant chignon and wore a belted smart looking blue shirt-dress. I paced the waiting area, unable to sit calmly. A few minutes later I was invited into the office. I sat next to the desk of an elegant older lady—at least she seemed old to me then. She was probably in her mid-thirties. Her demeanor was friendly and she smiled a lot as she looked over my application. She told me she'd once been a stewardess herself.

"I see you've travelled a lot and been around the world, that's wonderful. Do you really speak all those languages fluently?" she asked.

"Yes I learned to speak French while living in Paris, Italian in Rome and Greek because my mom is Greek but we lived there too, for four years," I said.

"Simply remarkable. Let's get your height measurements and weight."

I stepped on the scale and weighed ninety-seven pounds. I was five feet five inches tall.

"Oh dear, I'm afraid you're not strong enough to push those heavy bar carts, and the aircraft doors might be a problem," she said. "They weigh a lot. I'd like you to come back in six months after you try to gain a few pounds. You're certainly tall enough."

My heart sank as we shook hands and I left feeling deflated. When I went home I cried. I bought a blender and made milkshakes so I could gain weight. I drank a daily concoction of Carnation powdered milk, a banana and a raw egg. A teaspoon of vanilla made it palatable and I began to gain some weight.

"There are other airlines. Try Eastern," Mike said. "They're big and have a great reputation. And there's Delta. United. TWA," He was right. All was not lost and I'd apply to each of them.

Meanwhile we carried on with the hip lifestyle we enjoyed like two over-grown children who knew little to nothing about responsibility. We had friends we'd hang out and party with while listening to loud music, like Led Zepellin, Cream, Grand Funk Railroad, Crosby Stills Nash & Young, Pink Floyd or the Moody Blues. We'd smoke joints and carry on like kids who didn't want to grow up.

I went on my first camping trip when we took a road trip through the state of Florida. My favorite place was St. Augustine, the oldest city, founded in 1565. We had a small tent and stayed at the Anastasia camp-ground directly on the beach. The sea breezes and mild May weather had me hooked. I was awakened in the mornings by the singing birds. The old cobblestone streets in town reminded me of some places in Europe, mak-ing me feel very much at home.

"Wouldn't it be nice to live here?" I said.

"That'll never happen," he said. "No jobs. Unless you want to work as a waitress or something like that."

We cooked out at the campsite and smoked our pot. We met other like-kind people and made friends. They came from all over. Wisconsin. Michigan. Virginia. It was like being in a hippie commune.

I'm not sure when it happened, but I became tired of our lifestyle and didn't want to smoke pot anymore. Was I changing? It seemed there had to be more to life. But I ignored my inner voice and kept on playing along nonetheless.

Eastern, United and Continental invited me for interviews. It was grueling. Not at all like the National experience which was one on one. They were large cattle calls in big conference rooms at hotels where everyone had to stand up and tout themselves as being the best candidate for the job. The atmosphere of an audition, each of these events hosted fifty or more applicants. I compared myself to the others and felt inferior to them. There were so many pretty faces. I didn't consider myself pretty, just average. Never mind that I looked fine and could speak several languages. My inner voices were gremlins. How could I ever compete? They were so articulate and unafraid of public speaking. When it was my turn I hesitated, stuttered even. One time I lost my train of thought and stood staring for what seemed like eternity even though it was just a few seconds. That interview was a bust.

There was a process at United Airlines that stumped me. The interviewers introduced themselves and told us some facts about the company and then told us to take a ten-minute break in the room before resuming the process. When they came back they gave us instructions to stand up and talk about the people we'd chatted with during the break. I didn't remember anything substantial to say. I'd been very quiet and talked only to one person.

"I met Kevin and he's from Boca Raton. He works as a teller at a bank."

"Why do you think he'd make a good attendant?" the interviewer asked.

"I think he's friendly."

Rejection letters came within a couple weeks after each interview. I'd eagerly go to the mailbox only to suffer which lowered my self-esteem even more. I felt like I wasn't good enough. The typical paragraph began with "thank you for your interest…however you have not been chosen to be a stewardess at this time." American Airlines didn't invite me to an interview, no matter how many times I applied. I wondered why and I started second-guessing myself.

Was I really cut out for the job? Would I ever make it as a stewardess? I didn't relish working at a desk job.

"You'll get it someday. This is just practice," Papa told me during a phone call.

"You're intelligent, pretty and you speak foreign languages. And I want you to fly here and see me," Mom said. I yearned to see her again too.

My parents always believed in me. Why didn't I believe in myself? Maybe being in denial about a life that wasn't working at home, and living a lie had something to do with it. Avoiding truth and being unable to handle confrontation or take a stand to establish some healthy relational boundaries made me feel depressed. Airlines didn't want depressed individuals.

TWA finally sent me a letter inviting me for an interview that was held at Miami International Airport. They were interested in me because I could speak Greek. I was excited. That was the airline I really wanted to work for—they flew to Athens. I'd gotten "The Calling" in 1959 on that fateful trip from Japan to Greece. I was sure that this was meant to be. I'd fly for TWA and go to Athens all the time…I could do this for a decade or so before retiring. I couldn't wait.

I passed the first interview with a small group of applicants and we were each interviewed one on one. A week later I received a letter with a ticket inviting me to Kansas City on TWA for a second interview. When that news came I felt like I was walking on air.

The evening before my trip, Mike and I stayed up talking about the fun times to come. We stayed up late listened to Moody Blues music and smoked. The next day he drove me to the airport and I boarded the plane eager for the adventure that lay ahead. The trip entailed a stop over in St. Louis, MO before landing in Kansas City. A shuttle took me to Shawnee Mission, KS where TWA's training center was located. I was shown my room to be shared with another applicant. I looked her over really well, my competition. Betsy was blond and pretty. I liked her sense of humor.

The training center dorms were impressive, decorated modestly with shag carpeting and wood paneled walls. It seemed like a hotel that was custom made for stewardess training. There was a foyer that had large couches in a sunken living room for study groups. Betsy and I fell asleep chatting about being stewardesses together.

"It's what I've always wanted," I told her. She shared that she'd only recently decided to apply for this job, on whim. She'd just graduated from college.

The next day we had more interviews with flight crew and supervisors, and shown around the airplane mock-ups. They looked like real planes in a warehouse with interiors that had galleys and passenger seats. The interviewers showed where we'd learn how to serve passengers and perform emergency evacuations.

"A big part of your training consists of emergency scenarios," they said.

We were taken to a small medical center where our vitals and urine samples were taken. At the end of the day we were shuttled back to the airport to fly home. I couldn't wait for a letter to arrive with a training date. Instead, there was another rejection letter. I stared at it in disbelief. That one hurt the most. I screamed instead of just crying, tears flooding my eyes and cheeks. How could that be?

I decided to call and ask why I hadn't been chosen.

"Your urine sample tested positive for THC use—marijuana to be specific," the woman replied.

That was it. It hit me like an avalanche of bricks falling over my head. I knew I should have quit smoking that pot. That letter served as my epiphany. I told Mike I wouldn't be smoking anymore. There had to be a change in lifestyle if in fact I wanted to pursue my lifelong dream. That was the beginning of the end of our marital relationship. Mike liked having pot in the house. I'd seen people in our group of friends become addicted to drugs. That was not where I wanted to end up. I stopped smoking, except for cigarettes. At least those were legal.

We were at a public pool one day when I overheard two gentlemen talking.

"These two are leaving our company to become stewardesses at National Airlines," he said to his buddy over a game of cards. "We need to hire new tour guides to take their place."

I'd called National a week prior and they said the new classes had been filled. By then I felt like my chances for becoming a stewardess were waning. I was jealous of those two women the man was talking about. I asked him about it.

"When did they get hired?"

"Just recently. Hey—you look like you could be a tour guide and someone said you speak different languages. Why don't you come to work at the bus company taking foreign tourist folks to Disney World?"

Maybe this would be the stepping-stone to becoming a stewardess, starting out on busses. He set me up with the interview and I was hired on the spot. I happily gave up the office job I loathed.

I was only making $3.00 an hour but I was happy to travel from Miami to Orlando taking people through the Magic Kingdom. The foreign tourists were in awe—there was nothing like that where they lived. I also learned how to speak publicly on the bus and throughout the day in the parks. This was good. I was sure that it would help me make it as a stewardess someday.

Sadly, after nine years together, Mike and I parted ways. I'd outgrown the lifestyle and stopped being in denial about it. He didn't want to change or give up drugs. We wanted different things and fought too much. No doubt my denial contributed to this broken marriage. Had I put my foot down sooner things might have been different. Had we decided to grow up together instead of staying stuck in a bad rut, we would probably still be married like my sister and brother in law who managed to grow their relationships.

It wasn't easy to leave. I was scared. I scrounged all of my tour guiding pay and tips and found a small garage-studio apartment in Ft. Lauderdale Beach near the famous Las Olas Boulevard. Later a boyfriend moved in. But I kicked him out for being promiscuous and bringing women to my place while I worked the tours to Orlando. I decided that I didn't need a man in my life anymore. Maybe someday. Not now.

Months later I met and fell in love with a man who drove tour buses and worked in the office. Wayne was quiet and kind, and bit older. I saw in him a certain maturity that was lacking in Mike. All of my friends were married and having children. I was in my late twenties. I felt it was time to settle down.

We married and moved to Miami, closer to the bus station. In 1983 he gave me the biggest gift of all when I had a beautiful baby girl. I named her Pamela Rose after my sister and mom. I was so happy to become a mother—a change of mind from younger days when I thought I'd never want children. Pregnancy was fun. I quit smoking. I ate everything in sight. I gained eighty pounds that I worked hard to shed. Thus began my exercise habit of running or walking every day. I had a video of Jane Fonda's workout. I never lost all of the eighty pounds gained, but was content to keep the few left over on me. I'd been too thin at the onset of becoming pregnant.

I continued tour guiding, and enjoyed being on the bus and outdoors. The job required the type of energy I envisioned in a stewardess. I walked large groups of people around the Magic Kingdom and EPCOT.

In the late seventies and early eighties, the stewardess profession became known as "flight attendant". Unions decided that sexism would no longer be tolerated. More males were being hired. The job became known for being primarily safety related and the new title seemed to evoke a more seriousness, generating more respect. The retirement age had been abolished and a flight attendant could now enjoy a life-long career.

I re-applied again, to no avail. The competition was fierce, it was one of the most sought after jobs in the world. Airlines were still looking at younger applicants and I felt that at age thirty-one, I might be too old to start.

"You're not too old. Apply as a secretary. Get your foot in the door," advised Renee, an Eastern flight attendant neighbor whom I'd befriended. As much as I hated the idea of going back to office work, I agreed that it might be a good idea—a path towards my goal.

"Once you're in and after your probationary period, you can apply for the flight attendant job after proving yourself to be a good employee."

I passed the secretarial exams, typing 120 words per minute and was hired to work in the Frequent Traveler Bonus Program office. My job was opening and sorting mail from passengers redeeming points for miles flown—a new concept for developing brand loyalty and return business. I got headaches from the drudgery and boring routine. I missed tour guiding. The rush hour traffic put me home no earlier than seven at night—enough time to feed and bathe Pamela and do it all over again the next day. I'd start at four in the morning and exercise after eating a bagel with cream cheese. Shower, dress and drop my baby off at the sitters, then fight rush hour traffic to arrive at Eastern's 36th Street offices to start a new day. I craved weekends, which came and went with the blink of an eye.

But I never lost focus that this was a means to an end. It would be worth it, I told myself. As soon as my probation as a secretary ended, I shared my intentions with my supervisor. She was disappointed but encouraging.

"I envisioned you moving up in the ranks here. You're management material, Mary. You're a great employee and very knowledgeable," she said. "But if you want to fly, I'll give glowing recommendations. You'll be super!"

My office colleagues threw a farewell party for me. There was a large cake with handmade décor. It had an Eastern jet and a runway on top, with an inscription saying "Congratulations." The cake tasted delicious. It was an exciting time, but also bittersweet.

I'd made friends in the office and it was a comfortable situation.

Would I enjoy flying? What would life be like now?

Six

Boot Camp

I looked forward to starting flight attendant school, but I hoped I wouldn't throw up on airplanes like I used to. The six weeks training was grueling. There'd be two practices on real flights during the course.

Filled with anticipation, I read the Eastern Airlines flight attendant welcome packet over and over again. The instructions said to wear business-casual attire for class and have a valid passport. We had to bring one-piece swimsuits. I presumed that we might have time to lounge at the hotel pool. Clean blue jeans and T-shirts were also on the clothing list for other training occasions. Renee advised me to stay on campus because there'd be lots of studying and home life would be too distracting.

"You can go home on weekends," she said "It'll be over in six weeks." I didn't relish being away for so long and gave myself little a pep talk about how far I'd come—no giving up now.

I'd gotten sidetracked a few times too many over the years struggling to make a living working in stores, offices, and as a tour guide. After two marriages and giving birth to my baby girl, I now felt the timing was perfect to realize a dream come true and pursue a career I'd coveted for so long. I was melancholy about leaving my one-year old though. Would she remember me after the six weeks, and still love me?

I kissed and hugged Pamela goodbye and Wayne wished me good luck. That evening, I reported to the Royce Hotel adjacent to Miami International

Airport. The new recruits were paired up to share rooms. My roommate, Denise was twenty-two. I was thirty-two. The ten-year difference seemed non-existent and we became friends.

"Why did you wait so long to do this?" she asked.

"I didn't do very well at the cattle calls. Those large group interviews intimidated me. I hated standing up touting myself in front of all those other applicants. It was like—how could I be better than anyone else in this room?" I explained how I lacked self-confidence, and was once shy. "But being a tour guide helped me overcome some of it." I was too embarrassed to say that I'd almost made it to a second interview at TWA but failed the physical due to marijuana use.

"It finally all came together as I joined Eastern first as a secretary and here we are. I am excited now," I said. Denise exuded sweetness and had a great smile with perfect white teeth.

Day one was fun. My heart pounded and all of us seemed happy. I wore a black pants suit with a white blouse, and put on my usual conservative make up. I had a short dark brown pixie haircut.

We were taken to a small auditorium and shown a film about the history of Eastern from its first days as a mail carrier known as Pitcairn Aviation. I'd always been a fan of airline trivia. My favorite part of the presentation was a compilation of their old TV commercials. The best one was a clip of an Electra flying over clouds from New York to Miami. The narration went, "Fly Eastern and go from frost to flowers in less than four hours." We all laughed. "That's how come we get snowbirds," one of my classmates said.

The newer ads branded Eastern as the "Wings of Man," with new jets, Boeing 727's, 757's and Lockheed L1011's. The former astronaut Frank Borman, who was the CEO, talked about its wonderful employees' role in the airline's success. The ad ended with a catchy tune, "At Eastern we earn our wings every day."

That first day I thought about the TWA stewardess who had inspired me at age seven. I wondered where she might be. She must be retired by now. I wished I could find her and tell her what an influence she'd been but I didn't remember her name.

There were thirty other eager students in my class anxious to take to the skies, all of us with bright happy smiles. One of the girls caught my attention.

She was tall and beautiful, and had long slim legs. I envied her. I wished my legs were long. I started to pick on myself. She was perfect. She had a regal air, holding her head up high. She had long hair pulled up in an elegant do. I couldn't stop looking at her. She exuded the confidence I'd once lacked.

We toured the training center. Kathy, our instructor, was a petite lady in her mid thirties, with short blond hair, a turned up nose and a flashy smile. She was perfectly made up, and wore bright red lipstick. As she gave us our curriculum, she told us that we were going to be weighed at random. For my height of five feet and five inches, my maximum weight couldn't exceed 127 pounds. Even a few ounces over that would result in dismissal from class. After my pregnancy I didn't lose all the pounds Pamela gave me, but I was healthier than the 97-pound girl I once was, now weighing in at 125.

Many of us skipped dinner and sometimes breakfast too. How unhealthy in retrospect. I was often hungry. One gal was so worried that she carried around a little plastic cup to spit in hoping that the few ounces of discarded saliva would help keep her slim. She was at the cusp of her maximum weight. Miss Regal was as skinny as a fashion model. Some of the women resented her. Each time I weighed in the numbers changed. One day I'd be 123 pounds and then another time I weighed the exact 127 that I was allowed. That scared me enough to skip eating dinner.

Weight limits have since changed after a new set of labor laws ousted the old standards altogether. This led a number of flight attendants to binge on food after so many years of unhealthy eating habits and anorexia.

We were shown to our classroom where Kathy gave us our In Flight Emergency manuals that were about five inches thick. These heavy binders had to be carried with us on every flight as mandated by the FAA (Federal Aviation Administration). She told us that we would learn all of the contents in detail. I was awestruck by the enormity of the task. The binder was divided into chapters, ranging from Work and Conduct Rules to First Aid and aircraft specifics.

I learned the three-letter airport codes. There'd be a test on these and some were easy, like—LAS for Las Vegas. Some codes didn't make sense immediately. For instance MCO was Orlando, Florida. Many codes were abbreviations of the original airport name. MCO actually stood for McCoy, since the Orlando airport was once the McCoy Air Force Base. Ft. Myers is RSW—Regional Southwest. I used index cards as a learning tool like flash cards. Denise and I had fun quizzing each other for exams. I was glad I stayed on the premises. Oral and/or written tests were a daily event. We'd fall asleep utterly exhausted every night.

I had difficulty memorizing the location of each piece of emergency equipment onboard the seven different types of aircraft. We had schematics for each airplane type with diagrams showing fire extinguishers and first aid oxygen bottles.

There were detailed procedures for everything. We had to demonstrate how to use the equipment in front of the class. Each piece had to be checked at the beginning of the trip.

Retaining information for testing was not my forte. I hadn't been to school in a while and I envied the ones in my class who were fresh out of college. Learning seemed to come easily for them.

Homework every night was to read a section in the manual. For CPR certification we had a big rubber dummy on which to perform first aid and deliver live-saving breaths and chest compressions to jump-start the heart. I hoped that I'd never have to do that, but each practice built my self-confidence that I could save people's lives.

Miss Regal didn't want to ruin her lipstick to deliver the life-saving breaths on the dummy. Some of my classmates grimaced at her.

"What if you had to do this in-flight?" the instructor asked her.

"She's above it all, full of herself," I heard one student whisper to another.

Flight attending meant being firefighters and nurses. *Where's the fun stuff?*

We learned how to operate the doors for each specific type of plane. They were all different and heavy, weighing about 250 pounds. A Boeing door operated differently from a DC9 door. It took full body force to open and close them.

Next came the 'arming' procedure. Arming doors meant placing them in an evacuation-ready status so that a slide would deploy when the door was opened in an emergency landing.

"We *arm* the door after each departure from the gate and *disarm* upon arrival," Kathy instructed. We were warned to never forget to disarm the door upon arrival at a gate. That would result in an inadvertent slide deployment that could be fatal to anyone standing on the air stairs or jet way. And the plane would be grounded for repairs.

"An inadvertent slide deployment not only risks hurting someone, but it's a five thousand dollar repair, and results in a flight cancellation." I feared making such a mistake.

A highly stressful part of training was learning to perform an actual evacuation. There were specific commands and FAA mandated actions for evacuating a plane within 90 seconds after an impact.

There were specific commands to shout.

"Come this way! Get out!"

"Come this way!"

"Leave your belongings!"

"Jump onto the slide!"

"Move away from the aircraft!"

We weren't allowed to skip a word. Our actions were keenly observed as we performed in front of the instructors. The big dual lane slide on the L1011 plane was intimidating to look at from the top. The plane stood high off the ground and I was afraid of heights. But I jumped onto it. One student tore her blouse. I felt sorry for her as she tried covering herself up. I gave her my cardigan to wear for the rest of the day.

We started out with thirty trainees and ended with twenty-three. Everyone dreaded being dismissed. You'd be summoned at the end of class and were told to turn in your manual and leave the premises discreetly. Perfection was key or risk being cut.

The bathing suits were not for leisure time by the pool but for practicing ditching in the ocean. Using the huge hotel swimming pool for training, we inflated a raft and set up for survival at sea. Some of us acted as stranded passengers in the water and we were rescued by being pulled into the vessel. It was a chilly October day and I shivered from the cold pool water on that breezy day. But the rigorous training made me confident that I could save people. There was more to the job than being nice and serving drinks and food.

Finally—service training. We went into a mock-up of the interior of an aircraft to play hosts and hostesses. It was surreal. I was finally becoming a flight attendant. I learned to work with a bar cart and deliver beverages, and how to cook meals and place them on trays to hand out two by two. There was a retrieval system to pick trays back up and stow them into small compartments. It amazed me how much food and drink a galley contained.

First Class, of course, had its own procedures. I was fascinated by the elaborate service for flights to South America—Eastern's pride. They branded those as "El Interamericano" flights. We made the Caesar salads and carved the roast beef in the aisle on a cart. Dessert was a huge cake and we would cut it in front of the customers, serving it with after dinner drinks. There was fine china and real silverware.

We got assigned FAM (familiarization) flights. I was to fly to Los Angeles, overnight and return. Denise was on the same trip. I was so excited and thought I wouldn't need Dramamine, but brought it along anyway. On the first leg of the trip I kept running to the lavatory to throw up. I hoped the lead flight attendant who had to fill out my report didn't notice, but surely she had.

"Are you okay?" she asked. I looked at her sheepishly. "Don't worry—many of us start out that way. Do you want airsick meds?" I told her I'd take my Dramamine for the return flight, relieved that she was empathetic and wouldn't write me up.

A fun element for the girls' group was a visit to the Saks Fifth Avenue department store in Bal Harbor, Miami Beach. We were introduced to Miss Ginny, the Estee Lauder master make-up consultant for our makeovers. She was an elderly lady who was elegantly dressed, perfectly made up and looked like Zsa Zsa Gabor. I'll never forget her wide brimmed white hat with black trim and a black silk rose on it. She wore a long, flowing black dress.

"Ladies, some of you are not going to like this, but Eastern wants you to wear make-up for a professional look. Remember, when you are working on the plane, you are on stage, so the make up must be heavy—like actors," she said. "Always remember that your lips and tips must match, and that you must always wear nail polish. There can't be any chipped nails. Your hands must be perfectly manicured—you will be checked when you sign in for your flight by your supervisors." Lips and tips matching meant that the nails should match lip color. Impeccable appearance was the order.

We were painted up boldly. I'd never worn so much make up. I felt like I had plastic goo all over my face and I hardly recognized myself in the mirror and couldn't wait to wash it all off. I liked the red lipstick though and would never have tried it if it hadn't been for Eastern's grooming session. I still wear it to this day.

Our hair had to be off the shoulder, pulled back in a low pony tail or up-do but preferably short.

Miss Regal had a meltdown.

"I already *know* how to put make up on," she said. "And I don't wear red lipstick."

The next day her seat in the classroom was empty.

We were each being scrutinized daily for behavior and poise. Our hotel rooms were checked for tidiness while we were in class. I later found out there were spies in the training center's bathrooms to overhear our conversations.

We had the dreaded weigh-ins at random times of the day. We all groaned when, after returning from lunch it was time to stand on the scale. I made a mental note to eat less and drink half the glass of soda instead of all of it.

I missed my home and having time to myself. Denise understood. I liked locking myself in the bathroom to take a long hot bath to relax and shut off my anxious brain. I'd had enough of all the interactions and busyness. I longed to sleep in my bed. But most of all I really missed my family and my one year old daughter, Pamela.

Seven

New Flight Attendant, with Baggage

*G*raduation day couldn't come soon enough. Wayne and Pamela came along with my sister Pam. I was so proud to finally make it as a real flight attendant. It seemed surreal.

I made one last appearance check in the ladies' room outside the auditorium at the Eastern corporate office complex. Red lipstick fresh, check. No nails chipped—same red, check. Hair in place, check. I was feeling nervous but excited.

Frank Borman gave a short speech about the airline to an audience of about fifty people. Then one by one our names were called as we walked to where he stood to have our wings pinned to our jackets. That made everything magically official. After the brief ceremony we posed for a class picture with the CEO and our instructor.

Those of us who were based in Miami were given an orientation of the crew lounge and briefing facilities at the airport. It was a maze of tunnels, hallways and offices behind a secret door near one of the gates at Miami International. We learned the access code that only crewmembers knew. Past this door were stairs that led to the ramp area we had to cross to go to the crew room. The airplane engine noises blasted the air and the smell of jet fuel assaulted my nostrils. I put my hands to my ears to block the deafening sounds of the planes taxiing back and forth. Another door with a code granted access to the flight department. I watched flight attendants and pilots check in for their trips at a desk, retrieve paperwork with flight details and passenger counts before heading to a briefing room.

There was a protocol for reporting to work. The local crew schedulers showed us how to sign in at the computers and the other processes prior to taking a flight. Check-in, possibly weigh-in upon supervisor's request, briefing, then head out to the gate where the originating flight departed from. I was excited to be there, as I watched the flight attendants greet one another and go to their preflight briefing.

"Can you trade trips with me?" one of them asked another who was leaving the check-in desk. "I want to fly with a friend who is on your trip."

"Where does your trip go?"

"Los Angeles."

"Aw—no I was there last week. Sorry. I picked this trip up to do this Boston layover."

I was amazed we could trade trips with each other.

A supervisor asked a flight attendant to get on the scale for a weigh in.

"Ah geez! I just had a huge lunch!" said the poor girl. But she weighed in just fine.

New-hire flight attendants were slotted at the bottom of a massive seniority list that was in date-of-hire order. The newest grads like me were at the tail end of it. We began our careers on reserve status on standby and ready to fill vacancies when flight attendants called in sick or took vacations. Usually, new hires flew on weekends and holidays when the more senior people were off. We had ninety minutes' time to get to the airport once crew scheduling contacted us. We had no cell phones then. So on the days I was on call, I stayed home with my bags always packed, prepared for the phone to ring at any time. It could be for a short or a long trip to cold or a hot climate—always a surprise.

The day after graduation I was called to fly a two-day trip to San Antonio, Texas.

I'd never been there before and was looking forward to it. It was a Boeing 727 trip and I worked the rear galley for the first time, putting hot casserole meals on trays as the other flight attendants delivered them two by two.

I was exhausted when we reached our destination. The layover hotel was the Gunther, an old boutique hotel in the center of the city by the river walk. The crew took me out to dinner and gave me a tour. The river walk was lined with sidewalks and pedestrians strolling back and forth. I saw the Alamo where Texas patriots fought the infamous milestone battle. We had margaritas and Mexican food at Mi Tierra restaurant. The old market had a small rocking chair that I bought for Pamela.

"There's always room for flight attendant cargo," said my co-worker Carol.

"This job can take a toll on one's family life," flight attendant Paul said during dinner. Indeed it could I thought. But not mine. Even if it meant getting called in the middle of dinner time, or at night when I was ready to go to bed or the wee hours of the morning.

"This job will either strengthen and fulfill a great marriage, or break up a bad one. There's no in-between," flight attendant Mark said. This startled me, but I shrugged it off, determined it would all work out. I looked forward to going home and sharing stories.

But no matter how much I loved the job, I dreaded flying when I really needed to be home. It was hard to say good-bye to my toddler. I went to work when I was sick, saving my sick time to use whenever Pamela was sick. I had eleven scheduled days off per month split into two or three-day segments when I was free from being tethered to the phone. I made firm plans like doctor appointments or social events on those days. Pamela and I would get together with other toddlers and their moms and go to the beach or picnic at one of the parks.

Life was a constant series of surprises. But I wished I could pick my schedule like the flight attendants who'd been around awhile. Someday.

Those early days were challenging and Wayne became tired of it.

"When are you going to get a regular schedule? Why did you *have to* become a flight attendant? What was wrong with being a secretary?" I loved the job, so the very thought of going back to work in an office sent shudders down my spine.

What had I done? Should I quit?

Pamela seemed to adjust well. We had a nice balance of being together and apart. We were together more than apart because I wasn't always called out while on standby duty.

Like any toddler, her enthusiasm for life and chirpy talk brightened up any dull mood. She was in pre-school three days a week. She "helped" me bake cookies and cakes or fold the laundry along with other household chores. Sometimes I'd keep her home from pre-school just to be together. I had a wonderful nanny whom I paid to also be "on call." She was the elderly mom of a friend who loved children and this helped supplement her income. Pamela called her "Nana".

One day her pre-school teacher shared something Pamela said. "The kids were in the playground the other day and there was a plane that flew over us. She pointed up to the sky and joyfully told the other kids, 'Look—that's my mom up there and she's going to bring me peanuts when she comes home!'"

Life was good—except for having to fly during important events, especially holidays.

"You can make Christmas happen any day and have your celebration before you fly, or when you know you're going to be off in December. You'll learn to be creative," a flight attendant shared. Other flight attendant moms took me under their wings, showing me the ways to make family life as meaningful and fun as possible while at home.

In early December, we decorated and baked. I picked a day to celebrate Christmas, open presents and cook a big feast. The first year I was called out on Christmas Eve. New York and Washington layovers. We already celebrated our Christmas on the 23rd. Pamela told her neighborhood friends that Santa came to our house first because her mom had a special job.

When I got home I told her "I saw Santa and the reindeer. He passed our plane and was saying ho-ho-ho."

"Does Rudolph really have a red nose, Mommy?"

Christmas time in New York City was lovely. We stayed at a five star hotel in the upper Manhattan. I flew with several other reserves and we explored the sights together. I felt a twinge of loneliness being gone during such festive times, but the holiday lights and cold weather distracted me from thinking about being lonely. There was a light snowfall the day before. We visited Rockefeller Center and watched ice skaters as we sipped on hot chocolate. The tree was magical, the biggest I'd ever seen.

We flew to Washington the day after Christmas. It was beautifully lit up much like New York City. The hotel had arranged for us and other crews to have a special dinner in their dining room.

But as I took to the skies, my marriage was running aground.

We continued life as usual pretending to be happy. He was a wonderful doting dad to Pamela. I figured we'd get used to the chaotic life that my job manifested on a daily basis. Maybe by pretending happiness, happiness would prevail.

As a new flight attendant I was naïve. I didn't know what it was to be "gay" in the early '80's. I thought gay meant happy. I flew a trip with a nice young man whom I took a liking to like a brother. Jim was fun to work with and looked the part of a male flight attendant, polished down to the shoes he wore. One day we were sitting on a bench jump seat and he pulled out a magazine to look at. He flipped to a page of a semi nude male advertising underwear.

"Isn't he gorgeous?" he said.

"Oh yes. He looks like he really works out a lot."

"Look at those triceps. I like the bulge in his Jockeys," said Jim. I looked at him quizzically.

"*You* do?" I asked.

"Hmmm, yeah. I'm gay."

"What do you mean? Happy?"

He laughed, "No. Don't you know what 'gay' means? I like men. I'm a homosexual."

I was shocked. He was the first homosexual I'd ever known. But I wasn't turned off. I appreciated his honesty. We remained friends and flew together a lot. In fact, Jim was great to fly with since there was no danger of him hitting on me and we shared the same interests on layovers, like visiting art exhibits. Occasionally he'd help me shop for clothes and shoes. He had great taste for things like that.

This new flight attendant was slowly becoming seasoned to a diverse world.

I met Dee on a flight to New York.

"It's where I grew up," she said. "I love New York." We shared our backgrounds and both of us had wanted to fly for a long time. We became fast friends and sat on reserve together at my house because it was closest to the airport. We'd gossip over coffee and hoped we'd both get called to fly the same trips. On occasion it did happen. A flight had to be "re-crewed" because it had been delayed for too long and the original crew couldn't be on duty for more than fourteen hours. They'd reached the limit, so we took their flight out, as an entire crew made up of all new hires.

I noticed flight attendants and pilots having affairs, or one night stands at the layovers. They'd sneak into each others' rooms while thinking no one knew, but I saw it happen on several occasions.

One pilot shared with me that he had a home wife and a work wife. They'd meet on trips, spend time sleeping together and flying and then kiss each other good-bye and go home. Most of the crews acted as if they were in denial or were condoning these situations. That amazed me. I wondered how this type of devious lifestyle could ever work.

"Doesn't someone eventually get hurt?" I asked a co-worker.

"Sometimes it takes years, but eventually someone gets caught."

Flight crews came from all walks of life—we were a diverse group. Some grew up in the big city while others lived in the country and farm lands. I wondered how each one of them got the calling to fly.

"I was only going to do it for a couple of years," said Cindy. "But this job gets in your blood and I've stayed on for twenty five years now." Cindy grew up on a farm in southern Georgia.

Another flight attendant shared ruefully that she'd lost track of time during her career.

"I've been here thirty eight years. I couldn't sustain relationships while dating because of my crazy schedule. It's too late now. I'll never be married. And I wish I had children."

"I have no social life—this is it. My crews are my friends and family," said another. She was a city girl, based in New York.

It made me feel glad I married and had Pamela even though there were times I wondered whether it might have been prudent to keep the old standards of having to quit once married.

Maintaining a marital relationship was a challenge for many of us. But I would be remiss if I didn't feel that this could be a great lifelong career. I wanted it to work out because I felt I'd finally found the job that made be happy.

It seemed everyone had some sort of 'baggage'. I flew with moms, dads, single people, young and older men and women. All of us had stories to tell.

Working in the air generated high spirits among us. We were a family of our own for the duration, working as a team in service to the travelling public. The rewards we reaped were visiting new places and exploring the country and world.

Most of the time I had to pinch myself. I was getting paid to do this.

Eight

LEAVING MY HEART IN SAN FRANCISCO

I got called to fly to one of my favorite cities, San Francisco. It was my third trip to that magical place in Northern California and I looked forward to the layover. I packed jeans and a light jacket. The city was always chilly for a girl who lived in southern Florida where the median temperature was seventy degrees.

I checked in at crew dispatch and went to the briefing room where we introduced ourselves to one another and conducted a routine review of emergency procedures. None of us anticipate actually being in a life-threatening scenario, but we each took our responsibilities seriously.

Although we were going to be full, it would be an easy trip with one leg out and then back. The non-stop was scheduled for six and a half hours. We were flying on a Lockheed L1011, a dual aisle plane that could carry more than two hundred people.

"I wish we weren't so full," said one of the crew as we were walking to the plane.

"Hey—it's job security," said another. I liked that mindset because although it was easier to work the lighter loads, a full flight meant revenue for the company. The crew was a mix of new and more senior flight attendants. I was the most junior.

As the plane taxied she made funny sounds that were distinctly different from other planes I'd flown on. It sounded like wind passing through a narrow tunnel in a haunting way. I liked this plane even though she was one of the oldest of the fleet. It flew cross-country to some of my favorite places and I remember her and her sister ships fondly. I flew the L1011 a lot. Most of the senior flight attendants preferred flying the newer jets.

I worked a position in the rear of the wide-body. It had two aisles, two seats on each side and five in the middle. It was the dreaded smoking section. As soon as the "no smoking" light was extinguished, the cigarette-happy crowd was poised and ready to light up—immediately. The air turned thick into a hazy shade of blue-gray. When I'd quit smoking a few years back after I got pregnant with Pamela, it bothered me to breathe second-hand smoke, which made me gag and sneeze. I wonder whether we actually develop allergies once we clean out our lungs out after quitting. Many times I'd go home with a full-fledged upper respiratory issue of some sort after being exposed to the wall of bitter smelling smoke. But as a new flight attendant, I got whatever position was assigned to me, happy to work.

I liked my crew. Some of us made plans right after our briefing and decided that we'd dine at Scoma's on Fisherman's Wharf. I had the sole meunier on my mind and could almost taste the lightly battered fried light fish drizzled in lemon, butter and wine topped off with capers. We'd have some good crisp California Chardonnay of course to go along with the seafood. Then maybe after dinner a walk to the Buena Vista for Irish coffee before riding the cable car back to the hotel on Sutter Street.

Our hotel was the old Canterbury. It had beautiful large chandeliers and mahogany front desk. Persian rugs adorned the lobby. There was an old world smell—not musty. I couldn't place it but it reminded me of hotels I stayed in with my parents as a child. It was close to the cable car stop and Union Square for shopping. The cacophony of the cable car gongs was prevalent until the early morning hours. Ding-ding-ding-ding-a-ling-ding ding. The former city girl in me was excited to walk up and down the hilly streets and sightsee. It was a cosmopolitan place that was very different from the suburban sprawl I lived in. I missed living on a busy street like I did as a child in Europe.

We boarded our flight and prepared to receive the passengers. Being assigned in the back I checked that area to make sure we had adequate galley provisions and that the emergency equipment was present and in good condition. Once everything checked out, we told the agents they could send us the passengers.

The cruise portion of the flight across the states was uneventful. Beverages, meals, then pick up. The captain spoke whenever we flew over places that were interesting. The Rocky Mountains with snow peaks at the top where there were no trees. Bryce Canyon in Utah, a marvel of the world where the hoodoos poke up from the earth like sloppily poured sand towers. Passengers watched a film on the overhead movie screen. *Top Gun* starring Tom Cruise. Everyone seemed content except for a few restless people who walked the aisles. Every flight had at least one or two of those. I didn't blame them; it wasn't easy to sit for so long. They'd come to the galley and engage us in conversation. Usually the questions came like, "Where do you live?" Or, "How long have you been flying?" "Is this your regular route?" "Do you have to pay for hotels?"

After awhile I could later predict how conversations would start.

When we began our approach towards the SFO airport, I took off my flats and apron put my pumps back on. It was still daylight even though it was almost eight p.m. on the east coast. The sun was shining on the silver bird's wings as the engines changed their pitch indicating we'd soon land. I was tired but it was nice knowing we'd have an extra three hours' of daylight in town.

My thoughts were interrupted when the senior flight attendant called the crew to come to the front galley over the interphone. All of a sudden I had a queasy feeling in my stomach. That couldn't be good news.

"The captain has declared an emergency," she said as we gathered closely to listen. "We have to prepare for a possible evacuation. He said that the light-indicator on the landing gear is not functioning, so he doesn't know if it will lock in place like it's supposed to. We have thirty minutes to get ready for an impact if the landing gear collapses."

My heart began to pound—hard. I'd been prepared for this in training, but never thought it would happen to me. I immediately went into trainee mode under test conditions. The emergency prep ritual kicked in right away.

We synchronized our watches. Thirty minutes until landing. Each of us had a specific section of passengers to brief. The captain made an announce-ment to the people explaining our situation. Although he sounded reassuring, they looked worried. I was worried too, but knew I'd better not show it. It would only make matters worse. Be brave. We'll make it.

But what if we didn't?

"What if we have no landing gear?" one of my passengers asked me.

"Are we going to have a belly-landing?" asked another.

"I don't know. Please don't worry—as the captain said, the airport emergency personnel are prepared for us. We're going to make the landing as safe as can be." Pictures of Pamela flashed through my mind, skipping about happily, playing or peacefully asleep. My home. My family. Please God.

We walked up and down the aisles teaching passengers the brace position with their feet flat on the floor, hands crossed and holding the top of the seat in front of them and instructing them to cradle their heads between both arms. This was to minimize the effect of an impact. They gave us their rapt attention.

We selected able-bodied people, switched their seats with others and moved them closer to the exits so that they could take over should flight attendants become incapacitated. I briefed them with my instructions:

"When the plane lands, wait for it to stop completely. When it does I want you to release your seat belt and come to this door. First, assess the conditions outside. If there is fire, water or any other type of obstruction, this exit will be unusable. You must redirect passengers to another one. If usable open the door and inflate the chute with the inflation handle at the base of the door." I pointed to the floor and showed where the slide inflation handle would be under the door. "Once you pull the handle wait for the slide to inflate fully then instruct the passengers to come, leave their belongings and jump down. Don't let them hesitate, push them out if you have to."

I looked over to the one who seemed the strongest and said, "Once everyone has evacuated, remove me from this jump seat and take me with you off and out of the aircraft. Have everyone form into small groups away from the aircraft…" I'd memorized this in class and was reciting it effortlessly. I felt confident that the three men I'd picked for my exit were well prepared.

We were into the final steps and minutes of our emergency landing preparation.

The lead told everyone to put away all sharp objects and pens. "Place them in your seat pockets or carry on to avoid injuries."

As I continued to walk up and down the aisles giving instruction, my heart wouldn't stop pounding. I could feel it beating in my neck.

My innards were growling and I was terrified, but my face still didn't show it. Actress extraordinaire, I thought to myself.

When our thirty minutes were up the captain's voice instructed us to be seated. The lead turned off the cabin lights. It was eerily quiet except for the drone of the plane's engines.

I sat in my jump seat facing the last rows of passengers in the aft cabin and gave a reassuring smile to a passenger who was staring at me, a terrified look in his eyes. He nodded in acknowledgement and seemed to lighten up as he peered out of the window. I looked out of the tiny porthole window in the exit door next to me, not focused on the view, my mind racing. Is this my time? Please dear God. Not yet.

Pamela. Oh dear Pamela. I love you. I hope you will know how much I have loved you. I thought about my mother. My sister. Brother. Friends. Home.

As we approached SFO the plane banked to the right and I could see straight down to the ground. Tiny buildings. Streets. Water. Still maintaining a poker face, I shuddered. In front of me I saw faces of fear. People were praying. Peace.

"Brace!" the captain instructed.

"Brace, heads down, stay down," we shouted. It seemed surreal to be yelling the commands that I learned in flight school. This wasn't flight school. We were playing for real. I fought back tears.

The next thing I heard was KA—THUMP! The plane landed on its rear wheels then slowly settled onto the nose-wheel as it raced forward on the runway. Engines screamed as the reverse thrusters slowed her down to a taxiing pace towards a gate and stopped. The seat belt sign was turned off and the lights came on.

"Remain seated—do not evacuate!" commanded the captain.

It was eerily quiet as passengers gathered their belongings, realizing we'd made it safely.

They clapped. Some laughed. Others cried. I cried and laughed. I was mobbed by kisses and hugs, like a rock star might be treated praised by the people surrounding me. I had done what I'd been taught to do, amazed at how quickly the lessons had kicked in.

"You were so wonderful—you made me feel like we'd get out of this alive."

"I felt so safe after your instructions."

"I knew we'd make it," one of the able-bodied men said.

"You acted like a guardian angel. Your confidence inspired me!" said one woman.

"Buy the crew drinks on me while in San Francisco," said one man handing me a hundred-dollar bill.

We used it in the hotel bar for drinks before dinner and chatted about the flight.

"I don't need any more surprises like that," said the lead flight attendant.

"Me neither."

"But we all did great. We're an awesome team. We made it and we would have made it even if we had to land on our belly," said another. The three pilots were enjoying our hurrahs. One of them told me he was scared in those last few minutes.

"But I didn't have much time to think about it," he said.

"Well I'm glad at least to know that you're human. But you didn't let your fear get in the way," I said. That's how they're trained. Like us, they had a task to perform. Check lists. Trouble shooting.

Every time I landed in San Francisco since that episode, I remembered that L1011 trip and its faulty indicator light. The training I'd once hated that served so well. My belief in God and the power of prayer helped too.

My heart had never beat so fast. Perhaps I left it there in San Francisco that day.

Nine

NEW YORK NEW YORK

Whenever the phone rang, I wondered where my next flying assignment would be. Eastern had fascinating destinations. I was called to fly to New York with a long layover in the big city.

Riding the van from the airport with the L1011 crew, I took in the sights. There was constant activity that never seemed to stop. Frank Sinatra sang about the city that doesn't sleep. I could hear the lyrics, *"I'm gonna be a part of it…"* The driver whisked us to our hotel weaving through traffic like an expert. It was scary at times as he cut in and out of the lanes. Cars were going in every direction. Where were these people going? Everyone seemed in a hurry. Taxi cab drivers beeped their car horns at regular intervals, scurrying past us like madmen. We went over the 59th Street bridge and entered Manhattan. Someone pointed to the apartment where John and Yoko Lennon once lived, and the fateful spot where he was shot dead.

We checked in at the front desk of the Omni on 57th street in the uptown section near Central Park, and made plans to meet for happy hour and dinner.

"Want to go for a jog first?" Cindy asked. We shared a passion for running. I was eager to exercise on layovers, time permitting.

"Great idea, I'll get ready and meet you in the lobby in twenty minutes."

I grabbed my workout gear out from my suitcase as soon as I got into my room and made a quick change before heading out the door, not bothering to unpack completely.

Cindy was waiting in the lobby. We walked a couple of blocks over to Central Park and began our run over a long path that led to winding hilly ones. It was a beautiful fall day and leaves were beginning to turn different shades of yellows and reds. The air was crispy cool. A great afternoon for running, both of us kept a moderate steady pace.

We passed people strolling while others sat on benches observing the world around them. A great place to people-watch, I thought. Moms with babies in buggies and couples holding hands, young and old. I could hear several foreign languages being spoken.

Breathing with ease at a good jogging pace, I was thankful to have taken up running after Pamela was born. Not only did it help melt weight, it also prevented me from resuming a smoking habit. I enjoyed the jogs because I felt like I was cleaning out my lungs from second-hand airplane smoke.

We ran for a few more minutes and then I noticed dusk was beginning to set in.

"I think it's time to head back," I said. We turned around to retrace our route of return to the entrance. It only took a few minutes for us to realize that we were lost.

We slowed to a walking pace anxiously looking for familiar signs.

What if we never make it out of here? The thought of being stuck in the park all night sent shudders down my spine. Ugh. Weirdos. Rapists. Killers.

"We're walking in half-circles," I said. Cindy's face was anxious, mirroring my fears. I knew I had to get a hold of myself.

"Okay, let's think—how far did we run? When did the paths start winding this way and that? We ran on a straight path for awhile. Let's see if we can find that first path."

"I wish we had some sunlight," Cindy said. "Then maybe I could figure out which direction to go." I remained quiet. Finally we came upon a wall and walked alongside it back and forth looking for an opening. We couldn't find one.

"I'm climbing over it," I said, resolving to get out of Central Park onto the safety of a sidewalk next to pedestrians and busy streets. Cindy followed as I scaled the stony five-foot wall. Once atop, it was a shorter jump to the other side and I landed right next to a bench where a man was sleeping. My thud to the ground woke him up and he laughed at us. An empty bottle of wine rolled out from under his clothing. We ran back to the hotel as fast as we could, feeling giddy and laughing. We were relieved having escaped potential danger.

"Who knows what kind of crazy people roam Central Park at night? I didn't want to find out," Cindy said.

"Me neither!" I said. We were just a few minutes late for the crew happy hour gathering, so we rushed to our rooms to clean up and change. When we joined them we shared our story, amusing them.

"What are you having to drink?" someone asked me. I didn't know what to order. I didn't drink much alcohol except on special occasions.

"How about a Long Island Ice Tea?" another crewmember suggested. It sounded like a good idea. I was thirsty for iced tea. When it came I chugged it down enjoying the sweet taste. It tasted so good, I ordered another one.

"Do you know how many different liquors are in that?" Jim, one of the pilots asked. I had no idea there was any liquor in the drink and I'd just chugged the second one. I began to feel a little dizzy, but perhaps the running had raised my metabolism enough to handle the drinks without getting drunk.

Shortly afterwards we went to the nearby Carnegie deli for dinner. I ate a delicious pastrami sandwich that I could hardly get my mouth around and a huge dill pickle. The food energized me, and just in time. Someone suggested we go dancing at a nightclub. That sounded like fun, so the whole group of nine flight attendants and one pilot walked through Manhattan looking for a disco that somebody knew about.

The buildings towered over us. Living in a starter-home subdivision in Ft. Lauderdale was nothing like being in this metropolis. It vaguely resembled some of the cities I lived in as a child and young teen. Raising my head to look up was a dizzying experience. Every building was a skyscraper. Now I knew the meaning.

The entry into the disco was $20.00 each, exorbitant at new-hire pay. But I was eager to be part of the experience so I paid it. The inside looked like a church. Gothic. Wood dance floors. We got a table and ordered drinks.

"I'll have a Long Island Iced Tea," I said. The drink cost $12.00. But our pilot escort paid for our drinks and we were all grateful.

The drinks and the disco music made me want to dance and I didn't care if anyone danced with me or not. So I got out of my seat and started feeling the music, shaking and shimmying. Within a few seconds, the floor under my feet seemed to give way and I slid across the dance floor—on my butt, twirling, slipping, sliding and hitting the wall at the other end of the room. Embarrassed and humiliated, I got up, straightened my blouse and went back to our table. I wanted to disappear.

The crew laughed and told me to sit down. Thankfully, I felt like my "family" had my back.

I didn't get up to dance again nor did I order another Long Island Ice Tea.

I don't remember how I got to my room that night, but I'm sure that my crew family helped me. I remember washing my face and brushing my teeth before going to bed and then waking up the next morning with the phone ringing.

"Hey Mary—there's a Broadway matinee of *A Funny Thing Happened on the Way to the Forum*, want to go with us?" It was Cindy. Sure I would. I dressed quickly. We got the discounted matinee tickets and went to see the show. It was a great comedy and we laughed throughout.

Cindy, two other flight attendants and I walked the streets of Manhattan and passed through Rockefeller Center. There were ice-skaters in the rink and a pretty restaurant nearby. We walked past the NBC television studios. We went to Macy's. I'd never seen such a big department store with so many escalators, halls and elevators.

"You need to come here at Christmas time," Jan said. "There's lots to see here in Macy's but also throughout the city, especially the great big tree in Rockefeller Center."

I thought I'd ask scheduling to send me there anytime over December. I didn't want to miss it. Surely I'd come back to see more someday.

That evening it was time to suit up and get back to the airport. LaGuardia, which flight crew affectionately called "La Garbage". I wanted more LaGuardia (LGA) flights. New York was a place to have fun. I could explore it for hours and hours.

I did get to see it again several times. Eastern had many Miami-LaGuardia flights with long layovers.

One Thanksgiving I saw the Macy's parade with floats of various themes and characters. In December I bought a ticket to see the Rockettes perform at Radio City Music Hall. The Christmas tree at Rockefeller Center was the largest I'd ever seen.

As a junior flight attendant I got called out for many New York trips during weekends and holidays. Thanksgiving. Christmas. New Years Eve.

I didn't mind. I couldn't get enough of it. I loved New York.

Ten

FALLING FROM GRACE

I never knew where I was going next.

    Eastern's trips varied in duration. Day trips. Two-day, three-day, four-day and all-nighter trips, which some crews loved while others hated. Of course I had to take any trip that I was assigned since I was on reserve. I didn't mind. I looked forward to adventure, new cities and new crews.

One evening I got a call while we were having dinner to fly an all-nighter. Miami-Houston-Minneapolis. The trip had a daytime layover. The return flights, all night again, would return home at seven in the morning. I had three hours to get to the crew briefing. Plenty of time to leisurely finish eating and clean up afterwards.

"Sounds brutal," said my husband with emphasis on 'brutal'. "Boodle!" Pamela said, trying to mimic a new word. We laughed.

I was already packed. After showering and fixing my make-up, I put on my uniform, kissed my husband and daughter goodbye, got in the car and drove to Miami International Airport.

When I boarded the plane, I checked emergency equipment and supplies and sat in a passenger seat to look out the window since there was still time left before passenger-boarding. There was plenty of activity going on outside. Luggage trucks with strong men and women loading cargo and baggage. A fuel truck with a man wearing a fireproof suit attached a large hose from the truck to a nozzle under the wing to feed the plane. Catering trucks scurried about providing food and sodas to aircraft.

As I sat watching the activity, one of the pilots, Sean sat next to me and started a conversation. He had piercing crystal-blue eyes and an enigmatic smile. He was warm and friendly.

"Hi, I'm Sean. How long have you been flying?"

"About ten months," I said.

"Where do you live?" he asked.

He was good looking. Sexy. He had black hair with touches of gray at the temples. I was embarrassed as I could feel my face getting red. Did he know he was so attractive?

"I live in Ft. Lauderdale. Married, with a one year old girl," I said with an emphasis on *married*.

"Oh that's wonderful! What's her name?" He seemed to take great interest in me.

"Have you ever flown a Moonlight Special before?"

"No, this is my first time."

"It's not as bad as it might seem," he said.

I thought of Pamela uttering "boodle".

"I heard it's brutal. People sleep and we do a lot of nothing, but have to stay awake," I said, feeling my cheeks blushing.

"Ah, it's not too bad," he said. "I do a lot of these." We chatted a little while longer before he left for the cockpit.

"Moonlight Special" was a brand that was created as a low cost deal at $69 per flight segment, one of the first innovative low-cost initiatives for the airline.

"Passengers are on their way," the agent informed us. So we took our places to greet them, one of us at the entry door and the rest of us throughout the cabin.

"They look like the living dead," said Amy one of my co-workers as they took their seats.

The passengers came dressed in pajamas, hair rollers and raggedy blue jeans. Some jeans even looked dirty. People smelled like they hadn't taken a bath in a few days. There were drunks who slumped into their seats and immediately went to sleep. That was before there were rules to deny air travel to anyone smelling of alcohol or acting intoxicated.

I reminisced about my childhood days of travel when people dressed up to fly no matter what time of day or night. Those were the days of dresses and suits. Ties for men. Hair done up nicely. No blue jeans and t-shirts.

After a full day at home with my toddler, I was tired. But it was easy for me to catch up on sleep during the day at a layover. I could sleep anywhere, at any given time of day.

The flight was uneventful and most fell asleep while others read. Some smokers lit up one cigarette after another and bought drinks. The challenge was for us to stay awake. So we read magazines and did crossword puzzles while sitting on our jump seats drinking coffee. And having small talk about where we lived and how long we'd been flying.

"Do you have any hobbies?" Amy asked.

"I like to draw and paint, but I have a toddler so I don't spend much time doing that," I said.

We landed in Houston within a few hours, unloaded and refueled for the flight to Minneapolis. Our estimated arrival time was 8:30am. I was looking forward to the all day nap. Two nights of flying and a twelve-hour layover in between. Work. Sleep. Work. Brutal.

A blanket of snow on the ground and overcast skies greeted us in Minneapolis that morning. My eyes felt scratchy and my make-up felt greasy. I couldn't wait to get to my room and wash it all off and get the smell of nicotine off of me. I felt wretched until the ice-cold air hit my face and woke me up. I enjoyed wearing my heavy overcoat. That never happened in Florida.

As we all piled into the crew van that took us to our hotel, Sean exclaimed, "Bloody Mary's for everyone!"

"Not me. My bed is calling," I said.

"Aw come on Mary, we're all going downstairs just for one nightcap—or morning cap if you will," Amy said. No way. All I could think of was being snuggled up in clean sheets and a blanket. But when I got to my room I got a second wind. So I put on a pair of blue jeans and black sweater and went downstairs to the lounge. The whole crew was there ordering drinks. It was a party atmosphere. It felt strange since it was early morning. I didn't want to look at my watch to see what time it was.

Sean sat next to me and ordered me a Bloody Mary. More chatting. Flirting—it was obvious he liked me and it was mutual. I was struggling, fighting feelings that I hadn't felt in a long time. I was shocked with the inappropriate thoughts running through my mind and how my body was reacting.

We lingered in the lounge for a while after everyone else left. When I got up to leave Sean followed me to the elevator where he gave me a long hot kiss, his body pressing hard on mine. My head started to spin. Other parts of me came alive—and suddenly very wide-awake. How long had it been since I'd felt like that?

WHAT am I doing? Panic set in. And lust.

"Ding."

Sixth floor. He followed me to my room, walking behind me as if we had an unspoken agreement. When we got to my room we stood outside the door staring at each other. I knew there was no turning back then. I decided I'd let him in. My hands shook as I inserted the key and unlocked my door.

Once inside, we kissed before he undressed me, caressing me with a fever-ish passion that spiked my desire that much more. It felt surreal, like a scene in an old classic movie.

He carried me over to the bed where we made love with abandon. After what seemed like several hours of hugging, kissing and lying there quietly in each other's arms, we fell asleep. Then he awoke and kissed me goodbye before going to his own room. I fell deep asleep, utterly exhausted. No dreaming, it was a hard satisfying much-needed sleep.

When the alarm rang, guilt hit me like a tornado. My stomach did flip-flops. What have I done? I was *married*. What happened to fidelity—for better or for worse? But I needed this. *Didn't I?*

I thought about my parents. And my mother's advice that I should date instead of marrying right out of high school. "Get to know other men and find the right one," she'd said. "You're too young now." I ran off to marry my first love whom I really didn't know. And then I married someone else I hardly knew so soon after my divorce.

I was unhappily married a second time. It was the fate I'd chosen. All my friends were wed and it was what I thought I should do. Try as I might, I couldn't reconcile my actions. I was confused and knew I had no excuses for my behavior. I hoped I wouldn't get caught.

But it felt so good and I wasn't ashamed enough to stop seeing Sean every chance I could. We both lived within close proximity to one another in Ft. Lauderdale. We'd sneak away to hotels to spend time together during daytime hours. But one day he asked me to come to his house. His wife was away visiting family. The spark that I felt for him suddenly went away. The thought of seeing his house and being in his marital bed made me feel sick to my stomach. I'd struggled long enough with wanting to stop the six-month the affair, and this was the catalyst.

There were no goodbyes. He left to work at another airline as a lot of pilots were doing since Eastern was in the throes of labor strife and a pending bankruptcy.

While I felt a sense of loss for the excitement of getaways and tender moments together, I was also relieved. I was living a life of duplicity. It couldn't last forever. Sooner or later we might have gotten caught. I couldn't imagine the pain that would have caused.

I confided in another flight attendant, my friend Dee. She didn't judge me and always listened. I don't know what I would have done without her.

I fell from grace and did what I'd scorned others for doing. Would I forgive myself? I'd have to. I was human and vulnerable.

Many flight crews spent years in dual relationships. I witnessed heartbreaks. Some single crewmembers hoped their lovers would leave marriages and run off with them. There were affairs that lasted fifteen or more years. Sadly they'd given some of their best years living in false hopes. I didn't want that for myself.

"It's time to move on," Dee said. "Work on your marriage. If that doesn't work you'll find the love that you want."

It was a relief to fly free of the guilt that consumed me when I was seeing Sean.

I reflected on my marriage to a nice man who was jealous of my job and nagged about it too often. I wondered whether we could make things work.

Would he finally accept the career I so loved? Could we ever be happy again? What if we couldn't?

I reminisced about a flight attendant who once shared the profound statement, "this job will either strengthen a good marriage or break a weak one."

Eleven

SENIOR TRAINING

*B*eing senior meant two things at Eastern. You either had been flying for many years, or you were the lead-in-charge on the trips, no matter how long you'd been a flight attendant. To fly as the lead required special training— Senior Training. I'd always fancied the position. Some didn't want any part of it.

"It's too much responsibility. I'd rather just work in coach," said a co-worker, Sue. "I hate paperwork. And I don't want to be in charge."

I watched the seniors do their job. They had additional duties even before the trip began, as they'd retrieve the flight information at the crew dispatch desk. They conducted a thorough briefing and relayed the flight information that contained passenger loads and length of flights. The lead would oversee our choices of position on the plane. First class, or coach. Front, middle or back. The bigger the plane, the larger the crew and along with that—more responsibility. She or he would lead us in a review of emergency procedures. There'd also be a recap of service procedures. Each of us was required to bring our emergency manual and the senior would check them to make sure we had the current updates. Non-compliance was not acceptable and could result in fines to Eastern by the FAA. In later years, the responsibility for the emergency manuals fell to the individual flight attendants. This relieved the airline and if the manual was to be found outdated, the flight attendant received a $1000.00 fine.

The senior set the tone for the trip. You didn't have to like them, but you knew they were in charge which commanded a certain amount of respect. I admired their leadership skills. Most of the ones I flew with were amicable, only a few were stiff and bossy types.

"Let's sign up for the training," said Dee. "It's extra pay and gives us more options. It's another position we could get called out to do which gives us a better chance to fly since we're on reserve. There are some great trips that seniors call in sick for or can't fly because they have vacation time. Once we're qualified we could fill those vacancies."

I was intrigued, but not completely sold on the idea. I didn't relish the seven days of training. I was content to work as a regular crewmember. Once the application went in, my supervisor would have to give approval. I had a good record, and perfect attendance. So after some thought, I decided to apply and was accepted into training. I wasn't thrilled about sitting in a classroom and driving back and forth from home in rush hour every day, but looked forward to the training that only a few were invited to attend.

Dee and I sat together in class. We knew most of the material and we were asked to prove our knowledge by showing the door operation and other emergency scenarios. But there were some things I didn't like doing. One of them was extensive role-playing with one another with the instructors posing as our crew.

My scenario had an instructor who played crewmember looking disheveled and wearing non-regulation large hoop earrings that dangled below her ears. Her hair was unkempt and hanging below her collar and onto her shoulders, down her back. My job was to tell her to straighten up her image.

"Hi Jean. Wow, I didn't know how long your hair really was! It's so pretty. And I love those earrings. What are they, Chanel?" I asked.

She shrugged her shoulders and said, "yeah, thanks" as she sat down in the pretend briefing room chair. I pulled her aside with me. Never give corrective feedback in front of others. That would be embarrassing.

"Jean, I think your hair is gorgeous, but you know it's non-compliant to have it down and loose like that. I think you should put it up in that nice up-do I've seen you wear before. And the earrings aren't regulation—remember they're not supposed to be larger than the size of a quarter and not dangling. It might be a good idea to take them off before a supervisor sees them, and it really doesn't look good while in uniform. Maybe they'd look good at the layover with a dress or a pair of jeans," I said.

Clapping. Laughter. I was relieved that the instructors were pleased. Whew. Made it through that one. I was sweating under my blouse and my face felt red. Play acting wasn't for me. I was glad that was over.

But there were more hoops to jump through. We had a show and tell event where we had to stand up and talk about something that we liked to do. I talked about a book I'd read that was interesting, but everyone else seemed to outshine my presentation. Dee did a fabulous skit with Alf from a TV show. She was so outgoing and I envied her for that, admiring her spunk.

There were more role-plays between the 'senior and crewmembers'. One was about a confrontation between the crewmember and a passenger in which the senior had to intervene, diffuse and then confront the flight attendant. That could have been easy except that the flight attendant had been angry and lashed out at the passenger and the senior. There was paper work to fill out containing factual information about the altercation, date-time-flight and what transpired.

The senior had to learn everything about international documentation. Flights going in and out of the country had specific forms for each destination. There were immigration and customs forms for passengers and flight crew to fill out for certain destinations. There was a crew declaration that had to be signed and turned over to the receiving gate agents. This form listed the names of the flight attendants and pilots and the number of passengers. At the top of this form, we had to write the "block in time" –exact time of arrival to the gate – prior to deplaning. There was a cargo manifest listing food or merchandise that the plane was bringing in to countries. There seemed to be a form for everything and some countries had more complicated paperwork than others. Failure to have proper documentation could result in steep fines and trouble for the senior who was in charge.

We had to learn what items were acceptable to bring into each country. For instance the United States did not allow fruits, vegetables or meats from foreign countries and there were dogs to sniff out everything from contraband food to marijuana or hashish.

Forms day was so boring that I nearly fell asleep and I tried staying awake by having coffee during each break.

The final exam was another role-play that each one of us had to do alone in front of three instructors. The preflight briefing. It was to last ten minutes long. Not nine and a half, or ten and a half. The briefing had to consist of crew introductions, all key points in the emergency and service procedure reviews. We were only allowed to use the emergency manual for reference. No notes.

The day prior we were not given aircraft or flight information. We'd receive that information on the last day before the preflight briefing. Graduation would follow lunch, in the afternoon. We were all nervous. When I went home I spent most of the evening studying the details of each plane and various service scenarios depending on what route I'd be given to handle the next day for the test. I didn't sleep much that night.

Day seven was nerve-wracking. We went to class and each of us was called out separately to do our role-play after which time we were told to go to lunch. I was hoping to be among the first to get it over with, but we picked numbers and I was number eighteen out of twenty.

My briefing went overtime. When I finished, I looked at my watched and knew I hadn't passed the test. My heart sank.

"Mary, you did a great job but your briefing lasted eleven minutes. I'm sorry but we can't graduate you this time. You'll be allowed to try out again in six months," said Chris, the instructor. I was angry but kept quiet. Eleven minutes! Wouldn't that be better than nine? I covered everything that was important.

I went home feeling like a failure. There had been two of us who didn't make the cut. I was determined to try it again as soon as I could. I was envious of Dee who passed. She was very empathetic with me though.

"You'll make it next time," she said.

Six months later I was ready. Someone told me that the final test was still the same thing—a preflight briefing. I practiced at home, timing myself so as not to go over or under the ten minutes allotted. I had it down. I was going to make it this time.

And I did.

Twelve

DEREGULATION FALLOUT

"He's a rogue and a thief."

"Who is?" I asked.

"Our CEO. Frank Lorenzo. He's trying to break us; he's taking Eastern's planes and routes and moving them over to Continental. He broke their unions and now they can fly our schedule cheaper," said Ann, who was in her fifteenth year of flying.

I still liked going to work. But morale at Eastern was plummeting. I loved my job but soon realized I'd been in denial about the future of this airline.

It was 1986 in the airline industry. There was a lot of stress as a result of labor grief and strife. Going to work became unpleasant with each passing month. Passengers were irate. Flights were often late. Planes weren't being cleaned properly and smelled bad or looked shabby.

"I hate Eastern. This is the worst airline I've ever flown," a woman yelled at me at Miami airport as I was on my way to Boston. I ignored her. I loved Eastern.

"I've had enough of this damn mess," another passenger said as I was walking towards the gate. I avoided eye contact, feeling victimized.

I boarded the plane and checked for catering supplies. We requested more packets of peanuts. We were short by about twenty for a full flight.

"Sorry, we can't bring you any more. We're told to factor in no-shows. The company is trying to save money." Were they kidding? They weren't.

There weren't always no-shows. The plane would leave fully booked with all passengers.

I hated having to tell the last few rows that we'd run out of snacks or food. It was humiliating. But I kept thinking things would get better.

The plane had MEL stickers all over the interior, pasted by maintenance. "MEL" was the acronym for Minimum Equipment List. Certain things that weren't essential working parts for flying weren't part of the list, and planes could fly with broken seats, faulty light fixtures, inoperative coffee makers—just to name a few. Sometimes we'd leave the gate with inoperative lavatories, as long as we had the minimum functioning one or two, depending on the size of the plane.

The Deregulation Act of 1978 hit legacy carriers with a vengeance, and the fallout became evident. In earlier days, the government set fares and routes and there were very few airlines. Competition was scarce since each carrier had its niche of cities to serve. This enabled fixed ticket pricing to offset labor costs, fuel prices and new airplane purchases.

But the new legislation trumped those glory days. The deregulation act enabled "start-up" airline companies to flourish without government interference. The new carriers subcontracted their maintenance, leased planes and rented office headquarters—on the cheap. Labor costs for these new carriers were a fraction of what the legacy airlines endured.

What made matters worse for Eastern was the economy hitting a low, and an air traffic control strike that set a precedent for unions' loss of power. A mounting fuel crisis raised the price per barrel of oil to exorbitant levels. Profits were non-existent and Eastern suffered heavy financial losses.

All I wanted to do was fly, enjoy the layovers and treat the passengers well. And like any other employee, I wanted to be paid for a job well done which became difficult. I tried ignoring headlines in the newspapers reporting the grim daily outcomes of labor strife.

Our CEO demanded wage cuts and work rule changes. I was willing to sacrifice some things. But the flight attendant union advised us that they would fight management, whose demands were deemed outrageous—even if it meant going on strike.

None of us wanted a strike. Management threatened bankruptcy and liquidation.

I was scared. This isn't what I bargained for.

I hoped things would change, but didn't realize how big the problems had become. Frank Lorenzo had successfully broken their labor contracts and had a much cheaper work force at Continental. It was what he wanted to do with us too. Battles with Eastern's labor groups escalated. Lorenzo was ruthless, siphoning our lucrative assets and handing them over to Continental.

I was called to fly a trip to Boston for a short layover. Our flight was delayed as became the standard, marring the airline's image. The plane had MEL stickers over coffee makers and other things like a broken closet door. There were seats that no longer reclined; window shades stuck in the open position, unable to be closed if a passenger wanted to take a nap. "Inop" became a common buzzword.

"What happened?" a passenger said. "I haven't flown in awhile. This airline was primo the last time I went cross-country."

"I'm sorry. Things aren't exactly good around here." I started to explain the strife we were under, but he interrupted me.

"I know. I read it in the Miami Herald all the time. You people aren't being treated fairly."

Some passengers empathized while others blamed us.

"You all need to get with the program. Times have changed. There's competition and cheaper airlines out there. You're overpaid." I didn't respond. It was better to walk away than to get in an argument with passengers. But some colleagues weren't very diplomatic.

"How would *you* like to be told you're overpaid?" said one of the feisty flight attendants on my crew. "You're all full of entitlement. You want cheap fares and the best service. Well you can't have it all."

Another flight attendant took her by the arm and gently motioned her to walk away.

Was I overpaid? I work hard. When I worked I'd go away for days...what would fair pay be? I felt sad and beaten down.

The company wanted to slash our pay by twenty-five percent and make us fly more hours. The unions fought on. The flight attendant and pilot unions had had enough of the pay cuts in previous years' negotiations. There was no progress between labor and management. The machinists' union was the toughest, asking for pay increases.

My crew and I handled our flight professionally despite the shortcomings. We were getting more complaints than ever. "I'm sorry" was a common response to someone's disdain when I'd run out of peanuts. One article in the newspaper said we'd become the "I'm Sorry Airline."

Meanwhile new airline start-ups emerged and were flourishing. Air Florida enjoyed brand-new leased aircraft and low overhead costs, charging $69.00 to fly Miami-New York. Eastern retaliated by matching fares, but with old planes that were breaking down and high maintenance costs. Other new carriers offered a $129.00 fare from coast to coast.

It broke my heart to know the once proud airline I loved was no longer competitive and was financially bleeding to death. My job was in jeopardy making an already shaky relationship at home more difficult. My husband wanted me to leave Eastern, a company I loved, and the job I'd wanted for so many years.

The next morning we boarded the hotel shuttle taking us to Boston Logan for our flight back to Miami. There were eleven of us, nine flight attendants and two pilots. We were chatty from the effects of morning coffee.

"I've got an interview with Piedmont tomorrow," a flight attendant said.

"Me too. But not until next week," another said.

"It's a new and upcoming airline; people love flying them," the co-pilot added.

"I've applied at American," the male flight attendant said, "I hope to hear from them soon."

"Well, I'm excited to say that I'm going to Southwest," said his seatmate, our lead flight attendant. "I start training in two weeks."

"They hired you? You're so lucky!"

"Me too. I have a class date starting next week," the co-pilot announced.

I looked around the van and took in the excited chatter with trepidation. These people were bailing. What about me?

"So, do you have plans for interviews or class dates?" I asked our grumpy old captain, who was seated next to me and who hadn't uttered one word but instead stared out of the van's window.

"Nope."

"Well you must think things are going to get better then?" I said.

"Nope. I'm sticking around here long enough to bury this sucker."

I loved my job. But I was in fear of losing it by way of bankruptcy and liquidation. I began applying again to other airlines. Piedmont was having a cattle call in Greensboro, NC. I decided to fly there using my Eastern passes. I felt guilty being so sneaky but I couldn't afford buying a ticket just to see if I could land a job with another airline.

When I arrived at the hotel lobby and conference area where interviews were being held, butterflies fluttered in my stomach. Fear of past rejections flooded my mind. Would I make it?

Thankfully, my few years at Eastern gave me the self-confidence I'd lacked before. I knew the job and did it well, so I could speak about it.

I shared that I'd also been through senior training to become lead on flights. Piedmont didn't have such a program which surprised me.

"The lead position goes to the more senior person by longevity," the interviewer said. I nodded and smiled. "Why do you want to leave Eastern?" I wasn't prepared for that question.

"I love Eastern. But unfortunately things are looking so bad that I am afraid I might be out of a job and I love flying. I want to make a career out of it." I was sent to the medical room for vitals and urine sampling. Four weeks later I was given a training date and I felt as if guardian angels were looking after me to secure a job with an airline that had a promising future.

I thought training would be a breeze since I'd already done it once before. It wasn't. My assumption that all airline flight attendant procedures were the same was quashed. I had to unlearn old ways and relearn new ones. Completely different verbiage for evacuating aircraft. Same job. Different airline.

Graduation couldn't come too soon. I'd been away in Winston-Salem for training for five weeks. I missed my family and would cry talking to my five year old on the phone. Wayne drove up with her for the pinning of my wings.

I found out I would not be based in Miami as I'd hoped. This was going to pose pressure on my marriage and motherhood as I was going to be based in Charlotte, NC. I hadn't planned on that. Leaving home to sit in Charlotte as a reserve on call was depressing. I suffered days of just sitting without a call to fly. I missed home and my daughter. It was my first experience in commuting from Miami to another base. My husband didn't like the arrangement and I couldn't blame him. But I had to work. We argued about it often.

"I need to do what I love. Miami will open up soon and I'll get based there again."

It did. My assignment in Charlotte lasted three months and I was finally able to go home to Florida again.

Thirteen

MERGERS AND TRANSITIONS

I was happy to transfer back to Miami. Surely life would get easier now without a commute. My husband still wanted me to stop flying and work in an office somewhere locally. Marital counseling only revealed that neither one of us would budge. I wanted to keep my job. He could not agree with me. But I tried my best to make my marriage work regardless of our differences. I hoped we'd make it. There was so much at stake.

I was grateful for my daughter who was the focus and brightness in my life, Wayne's gift. He was a kind man and a great father to her. We had a small modest house where we shared family dinners and laughter. Pamela loved us both. But going back and changing careers to make someone else happy was not an option for me. I was obstinate.

The flight attendants, pilots and workers were optimistic at Piedmont Airlines. The upstart carrier was popular with its customers and emphasized service with a touch of southern hospitality. I enjoyed a good schedule and stayed home more often than not. A typical month consisted of twelve days of flying, but not consecutively. I spent my days off with my daughter and being a housewife. Three days, four and sometimes a week off in between trips enabled me to attend field trips with her class, or join other moms with their toddlers at a nearby park. We often drove to Hollywood Beach where I delighted in watching Pamela building castles in the sand with her friends. We had a picnic lunch, or got pizza at the boardwalk. We came home sunburned but happy.

Piedmont had a lucrative Florida shuttle using small jets that flew from city to city. There were many one-day trips that enabled me to be home each night. Typically those consisted of flying Miami-Key West-Miami-Tallahassee-Orlando-Miami. The routes varied and sometimes Tampa, Jacksonville or Pensacola would be substituted. Passengers were mainly businessmen and after awhile we got to know each other by first name.

"Hi Mary—good to see you again." I learned what they liked to drink and served them as soon as they took their seats.

"Here you go, Mr. Williams," I'd say as I'd place his drink on his armrest tray.

"You're an angel," one of them said to me. I liked being called an angel. A lot of these passengers were high profile local government officials. I once had a Miami Dolphin quarterback on board. He shared his fear of flying with me and was in awe of my job.

"You must be brave," he said.

I said, "My fear would be to get knocked over by three-hundred-pound men on the football fields all the time." We laughed.

But after many months of trying to get along, my husband and I agreed to part ways and to make the transition as smooth as possible. There was too much arguing. Breaking up our household and finding a place to live was daunting. I was scared. I was also wrought with guilt and self-doubts.

I must be selfish. I'm having too much fun. What's wrong with me?

I went for counseling again, this time on my own. Why couldn't I give in? Get a desk job again? The thought made me shudder. I needed to sustain a good income. Enjoying my career was equally if not more important. I knew too many people who hated their jobs and I was once one of them. I considered myself so fortunate to have the work life I'd sought for so long. But at what cost?

We sold our home and divided the meager profits. Dismantling it was heartbreaking as I kept on asking myself—was I doing the right thing? Would Pamela get over this? Would she forgive me? Would she understand someday? Will she hate me?

"Mommy why can't we stay in this house and you and Daddy just live in different rooms?" My emotions see-sawed from relief to sorrow. Anger. Self pity. Hope.

I eventually forgave myself, and made peace with the two failed marriages. I prepared to go solo which I'd never done since I left my home in Greece. But being a single parent was scary. Could I make it? I recalled Jack Canfield's words, "Everything you want is on the other side of fear."

We moved in with a friend of mine named Terry. We'd crossed paths at Miami airport one day. A Piedmont flyer who had also worked at Eastern, we became close friends, often running into each other at work. She was also in the middle of divorcing and was looking for a roommate. She took me in with Pam and even our dog Sebastian, our red cocker spaniel. Although our flying schedules didn't enable us being together much, I enjoyed being with her and her seventeen-year-old son whenever I was home. He had another friend living there, so Pamela and I were never really alone. We'd created a new family together, an alternative lifestyle. I have fond memories of one of the best Christmas times we shared in 1990. We bought a huge tree and decorated it with ornaments from our combined households. My favorite gift was a CD of the *Best of the Moody Blues*. Terry and I often ended evenings with a few glasses of wine and some flying stories.

"You're not going to believe the trip from hell that I just flew! Screaming kids and drunks. Those Orlando flights are craaazy! But the captain sure was a cutie!" she said.

"I just had the sweetest couple on my flight. They were going on their honeymoon so we gave them champagne. They got a little too kissy-kissy though, I almost wanted to throw a blanket over them." We'd laugh. Life was good. I felt free.

Childcare remained the same. Pamela went to her dad's or stayed at the sitter's house when I flew. Our family breakup hurt her, but she was resilient. She was a gleeful and talkative child. I engaged her in counseling sessions as well. The counselor was pleased with her adaptability. I was worried that she'd think our breakup was her fault. I wanted her to know that we loved her unconditionally.

But there were more changes looming ahead.

Piedmont was merging with USAir, which had also acquired Pacific Southwest Airlines, a regional carrier from California. The future looked promising but the Miami base shuttle flying was closed down. I was angry that I had to commute again. Did I sacrifice my relationships for this? What the hell! But at least I had a regular flying schedule.

I picked Charlotte as my base again until a reduction in staffing forced me to start flying out of Pittsburgh, Pennsylvania, USAir's main hub. I felt a sense of doom.

But as a popular saying in the airline industry goes, "if you don't like change, you'd better find another career." I chose to fly, so there I was.

I dreaded commuting to PIT. The sound of the three-letter designator alone made me cringe. PIT was a dingy old airport in a cold environment of constantly gray skies. But the flights out of PIT were good. I held a schedule that let me merge my life as a flight attendant and single mom. I still had to fly on most holidays, but we celebrated whenever we chose. My trips enabled me to fly up to PIT as it started and return to Florida after my last working leg.

I was happy again.

A new friend of mine, Tisha, had been in my initial Piedmont training class. She too commuted out of Miami/Ft.Lauderdale to PIT, while Terry flew out of the Baltimore base. Tisha and I began flying together often. We mostly flew up and down the east coast on a noisy DC9 aircraft with old galleys. Instead of ready-made standard bar carts, we'd have to set one up after each take off on a makeshift two-shelf trolley, which we'd stock up with soda cans cups, coffee pot, and other condiments. It was exhausting but we didn't care. Most flights were short and we had to hurry. In those days it wasn't unusual to serve a hot meal between Pittsburgh and Philadelphia—a mere forty-minute hop. On one occasion we were too slow. When the pilots announced we were landing, we panicked. All the food trays were still out sitting in front of the passengers. What could we do?

"Ladies and gentlemen, please put your trays under your seats—we're unable to pick them up before landing," I announced. The mess upon landing looked like a disaster. Tisha and I got on our hands and knees to retrieve the trays. The cleaners teased us.

"Geez—what happened? You have a food fight flight?" They had to vacuum the scraps. I was embarrassed.

We flew USAir's routes from Pittsburgh to Harrisburg to Philadelphia to Morgantown to Charlotte and then Ft. Myers before giddily flopping into our hotel rooms, exhausted. But it was fun. Pilots liked us because we shared jokes and we never complained. Sometimes there were harmless and casual flirtations.

"Are you married?" I asked one of them.

"Well I'm separated—by a few states—til I go back home. Ha ha." At times they tried their best to fool around but we weren't having any of it. We went out to dinner with them sometimes, but Tisha and I preferred spending layovers together in hotel rooms doing girl stuff, painting our nails or doing facials while gabbing and gossiping.

Tisha was my best friend. She unfailingly supported me when I felt I'd crumble juggling my life after deciding to divorce.

"You can do this. You owe it to yourself to stay strong," she said.

"I'll never marry again. I'm not cut out for it."

"Sure you will! You'll find someone one day—you're the marrying kind." And so went our conversations.

We spent mornings walking Hollywood Beach's boardwalk to sun ourselves and stay fit. Terry also joined us when she was home. The old "La Concha" tavern had a $1.99 breakfast that we savored. Tisha was happily married while hanging around two divorcees, Terry and me.

"My husband didn't like my job either," Terry shared. "I can't imagine doing anything else."

"Me neither."

We felt fortunate to have each other and the job of our dreams.

Leonardo da Vinci's once said ~

"Once you have tasted flight you will forever walk the earth with your eyes turned skyward. For there you have been, and there you will always long to return."

Flying was in my blood.

Fourteen

LOVE IN THE AIR

Despair and doubt dissipated. My heavy burdens seemed to take flight. Gone was the guilt for having 'that stupid job'. I was grateful for moral support given to me by two girlfriends and my brother and sister. Pittsburgh turned out to be a great base to fly out of. The trips were good and commutable meaning that I could fly up from Ft. Lauderdale in the morning on the same day of my assignment and fly home immediately after the last leg.

Pamela was adjusting to our new routine, and we spent quality time together going to parks or doing crafts and painting. I felt at peace knowing that I'd done the right thing. A dysfunctional marriage never proves to be a good example to children—she'd witnessed too much arguing and a waning affection between her father and me.

I spent the evenings before I had to fly reading to Pamela. Then maybe a Chardonnay nightcap with Terry if she wasn't out flying. I had a three-day trip every week on Tuesdays through Thursdays. I was home every Friday through Tuesday. Weekday trips were highly desirable and I felt fortunate to get them. They weren't always easy. Sometimes four or even five flights a day.

Work was a social event. There was a constant hubbub of activity in the crew room and in airports. I was continuously bombarded with the cacophony of airplane noise and boarding announcements. Quiet time rarely existed until I was tucked away in my hotel room at layover cities which I savored as "me time". After the busy days I craved time to relax and reflect or read before going to sleep. I went out with crews less frequently unless a layover was longer than the usual ten hours. Less time than that and I'd choose to relax in a hot bath and get some rest before the next day's flying.

I met new people, befriending some along the way. The career is not a job for shy people and requires a lot of energy. No wonder the airline sought outgoing men and women. I learned to overcome being introverted by consciously applying myself socially—even when I didn't feel like it. I learned to smile even though I was tired, my muscles hurting from pushing and pulling beverage and meal carts. I dismissed my craving for solitude. There'd be time for that later.

I learned a lot about diversity within the United States. There were so many cultural differences—and accents. I had difficulty understanding some of them.

"Do you have any playing cahds?" I realized that northeasterners didn't pronounce "r's" the same way I did.

"No sir. We don't have any playing cards anymore." Those days were long gone post deregulation. I reminisced about those days when we could offer amenities like post cards, writing pads with the airline's logo, and playing cards.

On flights from Nashville I had a hard time comprehending the southern drawls but I got used to tuning in to figure out what they were saying.

"Can y'all heeeop me with my luggage?" a lady asked me. I "heeeop'd" her put her suitcase into the overhead.

I continued with counseling sessions. I learned that I didn't need to have a man in my life to be happy—happiness came from within. Being independent was a new concept in my life since I'd been attached since my high school years. But I knew that someday I'd want companionship again, in spite of what I'd said to my friend Tisha. In the meantime there was no hurry.

I looked forward to the trips I was flying that had overnights in Ft. Myers and Boston each week. It was on a plane I'd never flown on before, the MD80. The trip seemed easy with long reprieves at night for resting or going out. I looked at the list of crew and didn't recognize any names. The captain's last name struck me as peculiar. It was Golly. What kind of name was that? I was willing to bet he'd been teased about it often.

It was on the first of those Ft. Myers/Boston trips that I met Captain John Golly, a very good-looking man in his early forties. When I boarded the plane none of the other crewmembers had shown up yet. John was sitting in the cockpit quietly reading his newspaper. I went in and introduced myself to him.

"Hi, my name is Mary. I'm the B flight attendant. I'll be in the back if you need me."

"Hello, Mary. I'm John. Nice to meet you," he said as we shook hands. He had a warm and tight grip. Friendly green eyes, an engaging smile, graying hair and a youthful face.

I went to the rear of the plane and put my things away before checking emergency equipment. What a looker. But did I see a wedding ring on his left hand? A few minutes later John came to the back galley holding a bag of popcorn. I noticed the ring and was embarrassed to have even the slightest attraction towards him.

"Would you like some popcorn?" he asked.

"No thanks." And that was it. The end of a conversation that never began. Passengers started boarding and I busied myself helping them settle in and Captain John went back to the cockpit. I'd bet hundreds of dollars other women and flight attendants never gave him such as cool demeanor as I had. What was wrong with me? I could have at least been nice to him and have a casual conversation. Maybe I was too attracted and it showed?

"You should give him a chance," one of the flight attendants later said. "He's getting out from under a bad marriage and he's a very nice man." But I stayed away from John during the layovers.

A couple of days later while I was at home I got a call from Tisha who was in PIT getting ready to fly. That was before there were cell phones. In those days we got prepaid calling cards and used the public phones at the airport.

"Mary—I met that guy John that you talked about. He's so handsome! And nice!"

"What did you talk about?" I asked, my heart fluttering some. My face even felt red.

"You. He really liked you. I told him we're good friends. You should give him a chance and get to know him," she said.

I flew with him again the following week and the crew went out to dinner together.

"I'm so glad you joined us," John said.

"Why?" I asked, immediately embarrassing myself. How rude of me. The question surprised him.

"Where do you live?" I finally asked.

"San Diego. California. That's where I commute from."

"Oh wow. That's a longer distance than my commute," I said.

He went on to telling me, "I flew for PSA – Pacific Southwest Airlines. When USAir bought us, they closed the San Diego base. Pittsburgh was my best bet. I just became a captain not too long ago. My seniority is good in PIT. "

I shared my story about the closing of the Miami base when USAir had bought Piedmont.

Such upheavals caused many flight crews to commute from wherever they lived to fly out of a base hub. The mergers USAir had just completed folded both of our previous airline companies into one.

"Where do *you* live?" he asked.

"I live in Ft. Lauderdale."

"Ah Fort Lauderdale. There was a time I wanted to fly for Delta and live in Florida. But they didn't hire me. I was hired by Eastern, but PSA hired me first so I went with them. In retrospect I think I made the right decision."

"Oh yes, you definitely did—I think Eastern is on its way out. That was my first airline," I said. "I loved Eastern."

"So you started over, with Piedmont then?"

"Yes."

He was easy to talk to, open, friendly and curious.

"Are you from California?" I asked.

"No, I was born and raised in San Antonio, Texas. Lived there and went to college at Texas A & M in the corps of cadets. Then I went into the Air Force where I began my flying career. I moved to California for Pacific Southwest Airlines."

"Oh, I *love* San Antonio. That was my first layover city with Eastern. What a fun place. My crew was nice enough to show me around. We ate

Mexican food and I saw the Alamo." I wondered when I would get the chance to go back.

I learned that he had travelled to many parts of the world where I had lived. He loved Greece the best. He was an instructor pilot in jet trainers and then ended his Air Force career flying a C130 transport plane. I was impressed, and had no doubt that it took lot of dedication and perseverance to do that.

"I love Greek food. We stayed in Glyfada, near the Hellinikon Airport, by the sea." He continued. A man after my heart.

"We lived within a couple of miles from Hellinikon airport, in Paleon Phaleron," I told him. "My dad and I used to watch planes take off and land from our balcony. That's part of the reason I love airplanes. He taught me how to identify each aircraft type. I've seen those C130's. Dad taught me what Boeings, DC8's and Caravels were. We used to make it a game. He would test me when one was approaching or taking off."

"That's impressive. I'm sure not very many girls really cared to learn how to distinguish different airplanes," he smiled. Greek food. Planes. Travel. What else did he like that I did too?

Our conversations took place on the plane between flights or when we went out for dinner with the crew.

I found out he was in the throes of a bad marriage.

"My lawyer said it'd cost me too much to divorce—so I stayed put." It was his second marriage as well. Another coincidence.

"Oh," I said, feeling disappointed. "That's too bad. I couldn't stay in a bad marriage unless there was hope. I left my second marriage."

I went out with him one evening in April, six months after we'd met, and we fell madly in love.

We shared so many interests and the same values and enjoyed each other's company. We loved our careers—and laughing together. He flew to Ft. Lauderdale to visit me. Pamela took a liking to him. He'd brought her a pink Cinderella watch as a present. She asked him to go for a walk. Took his hand and went off chatting about her school and the things she liked to do.

We often flew the same trips, but I felt we'd never end up together even though he spoke about it. I was careful not to place false hopes into something that might be a short-lived relationship like so many others had done.

Several weeks later I broke things off feeling that it was a dead-end relationship. I credit my wonderful friend Tisha who also thought it was time for me to move on. It was painful. I missed him, but I wanted more than just a flying companion. I wanted to be with someone who'd be free to be with me, without complications. Would it ever happen?

On my commute-flight home I listened with headphones to a song by the Moody Blues, *I Know You're Out There Somewhere*.

⌣⌐

Flying was lonely without John. Tisha and I had different schedules. And Terry was flying out of the Baltimore hub. I turned into a complete hermit on layovers. I dated a doctor in Ft. Lauderdale, but there was no spark between us. He seemed full of himself and his "things"—a man of many possessions that were so important to him. I was turned off by the materialism.

I flew my trips and enjoyed meeting new crewmembers while seeing the country.

Every now and then something magical happened in the air, like on a thirty-seven minute flight on a chilly October morning. Who would think that someone with a serious illness could bring joy to an entire plane filled with strangers? How many people can display compassion while at work, in such a way that it is a unique talent all of their own? Flight attendant Julia, that's who.

She possessed an angelic demeanor, and large beautiful smile. She had dark long hair. She clearly loved her job and passengers complimented her for doing it well. I hardly ever got the number of complimentary letters written to my supervisor as Julia did. She had flair and an aura of light. To fly with her was to witness someone giving more than one hundred percent of herself to her passengers and colleagues.

It all began on a short "hop" from Charlotte to Greensboro, North Carolina. A family boarded with their eight-year old son who has Tourette's syndrome. Timmy was about eight years old, and seemed excited to be on the plane. His mother told us that he might act up and yell. He'd been known to chant during the flight when he became agitated.

"It's his coping mechanism," his mom said. "If you try to stop him it only gets worse."

"It's a short flight," said Julia. "Don't worry. It'll be fine."

We took off with the flight being completely full. True to the mother's prediction, Timmy started to chant within minutes after being airborne.

He yelled out a word and then rhymed it with as many other words as he could conjure up for his young age. He began his first chant with "Ball", "Fall", "Call", Y'all" and it went on and on until he ran out of words. His voice got louder with each new rhyme. He appeared to grow more excited and began stomping his feet along with his chant. People were getting annoyed. Several businessmen were trying to do some last minute work in flight. Many were awakened from naps. We began setting up for a quick beverage service.

We watched as the strangers turned in their seats to look at Timmy with annoyance and confused stares at the odd commotion he was creating. Timmy's mother apologized to those seated near them and was trying to get him to whisper his "chant". I felt sorry for her embarrassment.

It soon dawned on the passengers that Timmy was a young man with special needs. He was growing more and more enthralled inside his own secret world. He stood up and was yelling at the top of his lungs the words "CAT", "FAT", "SAT", "RAT". Nothing would stop him now. He was on a roll.

I watched Julia walk up the aisle and stand next to Timmy's row. Then she began to add her own rhymes to his, joining him in his game. "HAT", "SPLAT", "GNAT". He began to nod and grin from ear to ear. Julia clapped her hands with each word and Timmy followed suit, clapping his little hands gleefully. What followed after that was magical.

Slowly, one by one, each passenger began to smile and add in new words to Timmy's chant.

One man stood up and started a new chain reaction as he yelled out "How about let's do "STAR", Timmy?" It spread forward through the aircraft like a wildfire, until the entire planeload of strangers were laughing, rhyming and clapping. When one chant died out, another passenger would start up a new word for Timmy.

"SIT" one passenger yelled. Timmy smiled and shouted, "HIT" as he giggled. Others chanted along with "BIT" and "GIT".

We chanted that day for the thirty-seven minutes from takeoff to touchdown. As the aircraft pulled up to the gate, all passengers rose to their feet and gave Timmy a standing ovation. One man said it was the most fun he had ever had on a flight! Timmy was beaming. His mother was thankful and hugged Julia as they left.

We all stood in the aisle with tears running our faces. As I looked around, tears were glistening in everyone else's eyes too. The human potential is endless. In just moments, Julia transformed a potentially unpleasant situation into something very special.

Sometimes a co-worker's talent shows up when you least expect it. The synergy between Julia and passenger Timmy turned a potentially bad situation into the best possible scenario. Julia used her talents in engaging the young boy. Timmy and the passengers made for great entertainment and fun for everyone. It was a potentially distasteful situation that turned into an inflight party.

Julia had the gift of being one of the most positive people I knew. There was always something different to look forward to on my trips with crewmembers being so talented and diverse.

One Christmas day I had a two-hour layover in Philadelphia. Snow lay on the ground. Looking outside the airport windows was blinding. Crews greeted each other in passing through the hallways with holiday cheer.

I yearned for the time I could spend holidays at home again. Would I ever be senior enough? Nevertheless, there was cheer in the air and my melancholy didn't last very long. There were passengers carrying big bags full of presents as they travelled to visit family or friends.

"Merry Christmas!" we'd nod to one another in passing.

As I walked the concourse towards my next plane, I spotted John in the distance. He seemed to be on a quest, looking for someone. My heart fluttered as he drew closer. He paused. Stopped. I looked at him. He walked over to me and we hugged. We had to be careful not to display the overwhelming affection in public. We were in uniform and all eyes were upon us.

"Merry Christmas," he said. I tried hiding my tears.

"I've tried looking for you. Calling you. You didn't return my calls. I'm ready to move to Ft. Lauderdale," he said, startling me. "Are you still interested? Is there still a chance for us to be together?" I couldn't believe what I was hearing. Chance? Of course!

We spent the weeks ahead planning his cross-country move. Four months later I met him at his mother's home in San Antonio Texas after he'd made the grueling drive from San Diego by himself. It was the same house he grew up in, in suburbia, a very different background from mine—the city girl who grew up in Europe.

It took two days to drive from Texas to Florida and we shared more stories about our childhood, dotted by long periods of silence over the open roads. What would the future bring?

Finally, we reached the Florida state line.

I became Mrs. Golly two years later on September 24th, 1994, adopting the funny last name on my parents wedding anniversary. Our wedding song was the Moody Blues' *"I Know You're Out There Somewhere."*

Fifteen

IN SIN CITY

After we were married, John and I weren't always able to fly together. But it didn't matter as much now that we could look forward to sharing our stories once we were home from work.

I had a trip to Las Vegas, another favorite city. It was a long flight from the east coast, so when I'd get there I didn't stay out as late as some of the younger crews did. A few hours trying my luck at gambling and then dinner would suit me fine. After that a hot bath and bed.

When the phone rang in my hotel room the next morning, I was startled. Maybe it was the captain to tell me there was a delay going back. Or perhaps it was crew scheduling, to say we were being rerouted. Things like that could happen when the weather somewhere affected the flying patterns and crews had switch flights.

"Hello?" I answered with anticipation. I was lazily enjoying my first cup of coffee anticipating going home later. I liked longer overnights like these. No early wake-up alarms.

"Hi Mary. It's Joe," said the captain. "I'm just calling to let you know that one of our flight attendants, Judy, won't be flying the rest of the trip with us. She called off. Scheduling is working on a replacement."

"Oh. Okay. Is she all right?" I asked.

"Well, let's just say she's…I think she's indisposed. It's complicated. I'll tell you later. Are you going downstairs for breakfast this morning?"

"I was planning to…in about an hour or so." I said.

"Okay, I'll see you down there then."

What could possibly have happened? When we arrived the night prior, it had been a long flight from Charlotte. The passengers kept us running. More drinks. A *lot* of drinks. Flights to Las Vegas were always like that. People were in party mode. Loud. High maintenance is what we called it. It wasn't unusual to order several doubles of mixed concoctions from the bar cart. They would start their vacation with a bang. Five hours of flying and running back and forth with the tray could be exhausting, but thankfully I'd gotten a good night's sleep and felt refreshed for the flight back.

I finished my coffee and brewed another in the room's coffee maker. It wasn't the best, but I enjoyed staying in my pajamas while having a few cups in bed. I'd read, or watch the news then go to breakfast. I was intrigued by what the captain's news might be about Judy. I hoped she was okay.

The lobby was already crowded with gamblers. The machines jingled and clanged with pennies, nickels and dimes. It was ten thirty and some folks were already drinking. There were women who were overly made up, and had hair dyed in oranges, reds and browns that didn't look natural. Some were dressed in full regalia of glitz and bling. There were men in jeans and cowboy hats, and others looked like they were trying to look like Elvis. A drunk woman stumbled into the elevator with someone who was holding her upright, chuckling at her. Poor thing. She needed bed and sleep. Waitresses wearing fishnet hose, very short black shorts and low cut tops with protruding coconut-like boobs wandered about with trays of drinks to deliver to people who were placing bets at tables. I couldn't figure out how they placed bets without a clear mind. Slot machines were random and mindless, but card games? That required some thinking. How ironic that the name of this hotel was "Terribles." It was located on Tropicana Avenue, a few blocks from the strip. It really was—kind of terrible. They allowed smoking in the casino that was in the main lobby. Every time I passed through it I gagged, sneezed and my eyes watered. But they served a savory breakfast twenty-four hours a day that only cost $2.99. I made my way to the upstairs restaurant, feeling a little out of place in my sweats and sneakers.

Captain Joe was sitting there waiting for me. He was with his first officer, the second pilot on our trip.

"Come, sit," Joe beckoned. The waitress offered me a menu and some coffee. It smelled good, a lot better than the stuff I had in my room. I ordered some orange juice and an omelette.

"So, what happened to Judy?" I asked Joe.

Both pilots shifted in their chairs. Be still, the rest of it will be forthcoming, I thought as I waited patiently.

"We went to the steak place I mentioned last night. It was good food—wish you'd have come with us. Had drinks and dinner. Then Chris (one of the other flight attendants) suggested we go for after dinner drinks at some place on the strip. It was all good fun." He said.

Okay. Cut to the chase. I'd had enough of the suspense already. But I continued to sit still as I listened.

"Well, with all the drinking at the restaurant, when we got to this other place, Judy decided she wanted a martini. Yeah, a *martini*," he said. "As if she hadn't had enough alcohol already, she picked a drink that was lethal."

"When we left, we walked past this strip joint. Judy was curious. She said she'd never been to one before. She begged us to take her in. I told her it wasn't a good idea."

Oh boy. This is getting interesting. Why would she want to do that?

Joe continued, "Well, we went in."

Of course. She *begged* them, right? I shook my head as I looked over at the first officer, Randy. He didn't seem amused. And as Joe was relating the story, I got the feeling the story would worsen.

"Okay, so what happened?" I asked finally, after what seemed like too long a period of silence.

It was Randy who responded. "It was amateur night. Judy wanted a chance to show her stuff and be a stripper."

I looked at both of them, shaking my head. "Oh no." That was risky stuff. Brave too.

"We tried to talk her out of it. Begged her, in fact. She wouldn't listen. I even went as far as to ask her what her kids would think, or husband for that matter."

"And?"

"She insisted. Chris even tried to forcefully walk her out of the place, but there was no stopping Judy. She was determined to do it." I remembered Judy during the flight. She was outgoing, flirty and seemed like a fun-loving free spirit. I liked her.

"You didn't leave her there did you?" I asked.

"Oh no. She went to the dressing room, got into some sexy bikini thongy kind of gear and came out and, I must say she was pretty good, gorgeous gal that she is…" he trailed off. "Then she began taking it all off. She was quite popular—got lots of attention from the guys. They were tipping her well."

Randy continued. "We got her out of there as soon as she got her clothes on and cabbed it back to the hotel. She was real tipsy and was stoked that she got to do that, saying it was her opportunity of a lifetime to be a stripper for a few minutes—a fantasy she'd had for years. Her fifteen minutes of fame, if you will."

"But this morning, she must have woken up with remorse." Joe said. "I was wondering about that—whether she'd still feel so up about it the next day. How she'd face us. I felt sorry for her. I really tried to get her out of there, tried to talk her out of it. I feel responsible in some way—we probably shouldn't have even gone there."

"No maybe you shouldn't have. But she's a grown girl. She should have known better too." I said, trying to alleviate some of Joe's, Randy's and probably Chris's guilt too. Maybe if I'd gone…there would have been a different outcome. But maybe not.

"Scheduling called me this morning to say she'd called off sick. Maybe she was sick after all the drinking, tiny girl that she is—except for her boobs, they weren't tiny by any means. We probably should leave it at that. I hesitated telling you, but it might come up at some point and it would be good for you to know the truth."

I wondered how poor Judy was feeling. Was she hung over? Did she feel embarrassed? I wished there was a way I could get in touch with her.

"How about if we keep this our secret. It doesn't get out to anyone. Are we all onboard with this?" I asked them. I felt sorry for her.

"Yeah," said Joe. "I guess that's why they call this place Sin City."

Sixteen

RECURRENT NIGHTMARE

"Release seats belts! Get out!" I yelled, looking through the porthole of the aircraft door, to assess outdoor conditions.

"Stand back! Stand back!" I opened the exit to reach the inflation handle that would render a usable escape slide. *Ppsssshhhhhh*. Slide inflated. Get them out now.

"Come this way—jump!…"

My performance was the same every year. It was second nature. I knew how to evacuate people safely within ninety seconds as soon as the captain gave the command to start. I'd practiced it enough times before class, and dreamed about it the night before.

A puzzled look emanated from my instructor's otherwise poker face.

"Did you watch the online videos?" she asked.

I'd looked at them on the employee website, and spent six long hours reviewing emergency evacuation scenarios for each aircraft type that I flew. All seven of them.

"Yes, I did."

"Did you notice that, when opening this door in emergency mode, you are no longer supposed to use both hands?" I shook my head. "Okay—no worries. You'll get it on the second go 'round." She scribbled something next to my name as she waited for my next try.

Such was my first hour in Recurrent Training—the FAA mandated event that recertified thousands of flight attendants every year. We dreaded it, fretted and spoke about it for days beforehand. I didn't know any flight attendants who enjoyed it. We gave this an acronym too: YBYJ—"you bet your job." It was a long, stressful day full of drills and scenarios and written tests and lists of acronyms. The POB was the portable oxygen bottle, for instance. The PBE, protective breathing equipment for fighting fires. The FAK, first aid kit.

Two tries were the maximum allowed to pass the evacuation process. If the second try wasn't at one hundred percent proficiency, there's one last chance at the end of the eight-hour day to redo it from start to finish. The pressure was on me now. Doing it over is one thing. Dwelling on it all day long—no—I didn't need it to get that far. Please…dear God. Okay, I was going to get it right this time. Take two…

My heart pumped fast with my adrenaline running at top speed. It was nerve-wracking enough to be shouting commands at each aircraft trainer door, verbatim, and not forget any details, verbal, or physical actions. I took a deep breath. No repeat after this. I can do it.

But ingrained habits be damned, I didn't make it and would have to do it again at the end of the day. It wasn't the first time. I'd made mistakes before over the previous thirty years. It needed to be perfect—including that one darned right hand behind my back. Crap! When did that change? How did I miss it? Apparently a crewmember had injured her right arm at this door. Measures were taken to avoid this ever happening again.

"It's more than just about serving drinks and food," I told a neighbor who asked why we had to perform at this yearly event. "We're safety professionals and it's always good to review and practice. It's about maintaining proficiency."

I breezed through the rest it, performing CPR (cardiopulmonary resuscitation) on a big rubber dummy; demonstrating my knowledge in the use of the heart defibrillator. Then self-defense techniques on another rubber dummy that was standing in front of me looking mean—I envisioned him being a hijacker trying to get into the cockpit. I hit him hard and poked his eyes with my fingers, taking out my frustration for having to repeat the 757 evacuation later. I hoped I'd never have an incident like a hijacking. But we had to be prepared for it.

There were fire-fighting procedures. Which fire extinguisher to use would be determined by the type of fire, electrical, cloth or paper? But remember to put on protective breathing equipment first—another bad mark if we forget. And then there was the cabin prep scenario—in which a pretend captain called on the interphone to tell you there was going to be an emergency landing.

"What's the nature of the emergency?" I asked.

"We have a fire in the right engine."

"How much time do I have to prepare the cabin?"

"We'll be landing in fifteen minutes. I'll tell you when to brace for impact. Let me know as soon as you are all ready."

"Yes sir." I looked at my watch.

As the designated lead, I proceeded to brief the rest of my crew. We synchronized our watches. We briefed our pretend passengers on how to get into a brace position, what to do and where to exit once we landed and what to do if a flight attendant was incapacitated. As we went through the process in the fifteen-minute time frame, I was confident that we were all ready to survive a catastrophe. It was a good exercise in review.

There was very little training in recurrent. We were supposed to know our stuff, and show how well we knew it, or learn from our mistakes. After each scenario there was a debriefing, with feedback. If we weren't receptive, or had difficulty learning, there was "target training" specifically designed as remedial learning in which we'd have to come back the next day. Target training was nobody's desire of course—the thought of it was dreadful. I'd heard it entailed repetitive practice and even more testing.

Oh my God, I've got to pass when I do that 757 door again. This weighed on my mind throughout the day.

Will I make my Brussels trip tomorrow? I'll be in a mess if I don't get it done right. I've got to quit thinking like that. I'll be fine. I'm going to make a hundred percent....

I knew I would. But my mind drifted to the dreaded outcome, fear rearing its ugly head. I had to give up the *"what if I fail?"* mindset. I started thinking about that poster in the Discovery seminar that said, *"What I fear, I create".*

I couldn't wait until it was over.

"You're gonna ace it," Tisha said me with great conviction over lunch. I barely chewed my sandwich. I think I inhaled it.

God bless my best friend. She was always there for me. We were there for each other. We'd taken this training together every year for moral support. It turned into a girls' event, sharing a hotel room the night prior, where we'd hang out in our pajamas and put mud masks on our faces and share funny stories. Of course we did some studying as well.

There was more role-playing in the afternoon. We had a pseudo 'decompression' in flight, where we shouted commands at passengers to put on their masks that dropped down in the mock plane. Another scenario had an instructor acting out as an irate and pesky passenger to see how we'd handle the situation. He missed his calling. He should have been an actor. It was hard not to laugh in the process. He pestered, and kept nudging us for his attention.

He demanded his coffee *"right now,"* agitating everyone around him.

"Hey, move over, take your elbow off *my* armrest." He yelled at his seatmate.

"Sir, you are getting loud and disturbing people around you," I warned.

"But he's in my space. And why are *you* bothering me? You're nothing but a waitress. Leave me alone. I don't like you. This coffee sucks. I'll never fly this airline again." He went on and on, stirring up a ruckus with others around him. Shouting.

I was "it," so I addressed our perpetrator.

"Sir, you have created several disruptions today and I must bring to your attention that should this go any further, we will have authorities meet you upon landing. You will be arrested for misconduct..." and I showed him the report form I would have to use.

"Cut! Stop the scenario," another instructor said.

Applause. Laughter. Debrief. Feedback.

Onto the next module. Will this day ever be over?

We went over in flight paperwork. Yawn. I need coffee.

At the end of the day it was water-ditching time. We climbed into a large raft, erected a musty smelling canopy and sat under the stinky thing while we reviewed how to deploy a sea anchor. One of us had to open up the survival kit and show the sea dye markers which tinted the water, and the flares that make us visible for rescuers to identify our location. More review. The cynic in me wondered how on earth one could survive a water landing. Believe, I told myself. Just believe you can. And I knew I could. Flight attendants could do so much more than smile and serve food and beverages. We are life savers.

My mind went adrift. Each year I hoped I'd never have any of this really happen. Years later there was a water ditching on the Hudson River when one of our own Captain "Sully" Sullenberger's expertise landed safely on the water. He had to glide the plane down when both engines were lost to the geese they'd ingested. There'd been no fatalities. I was proud of the flight attendants who knew their ditching procedures and evacuated the aircraft swiftly. They too sat in a raft once and worked the same trainer doors. Their lessons kicked in as they were meant to do. Which is why we were doing it every year.

Finally, class was dismissed. Tisha squeezed my hand and gave me her knowing look that I'd kick ass at that stupid 757 door exit. And I did.

When I met her in the lobby we did our 'woohoo' high five with big hugs before getting on the shuttle to the airport.

Enormous relief swept over me.

"We did it again, just like we always do!" Tisha said. "You bet your job and won!" she laughed. Finally—it was over.

At the airport, we went into celebration ritual. Time to order a martini, click glasses and cheer ourselves for another successful venture and a new year ahead.

I went to Philly to spend the night before taking my trip out the next day and took a long, hot bath. It felt soothing to my sore muscles. The aircraft doors and windows were always heavy to lift, push or pull. I was in great shape, since I worked out frequently, but this was different, and the adrenaline expenditure of the day had depleted me. I slept soundly pushing nightmares aside.

Every year was different and I soon learned to embrace the training. The more I did, the better the results.

*C*heck-in time for my next day's trip was early afternoon. I slept in and woke up feeling refreshed and happy.

The preflight briefing was the perfunctory standard and as I looked around at my crew, I felt a sense of gratitude for the previous day. It was the annual rite of passage that prepared me for whatever might possibly happen out of the ordinary.

We boarded a full flight, left the gate, taxied out and took off without incident and performed all of our duties with smiles and pleasantries. We were a cheerful bunch. After the first part of the service was over however, chaos erupted on the other side of the dual aisle wide body plane. I looked over and saw two passengers who seemed to be at odds with one another.

Oh no. Not now.

Things had been going so nice and smoothly.

"Hey Mary, we need you to talk to these people. They're speaking French."

They were cussing at each other by the time I reached their seats. This was no pretend scenario. But it was like—déjà vu. I had the Passenger Misconduct Report form in my tote bag. I'd had the practice and I was ready.

"Sir. What is the problem?" I asked one of the two grown men.

"Well theees personn is not leeessening to me. He is taking his seat and poooting it een my face!" Oh dear, a seatback issue, and they're acting like children. Really.

"No no, monsieur. My seat ees reclining, just like yours does. Eeeess sappost to. I want to sleep. It eeez my right to recline my seat!"

"Excuse me, both of you. This is disruptive. You are being loud and annoying people around you who want peace and quiet and want to sleep. I will have to tell the Captain to call the authorities to the plane when we land if we have any more of this behavior. Please help each other out and be nice."

Silence. They complied, deciding to ignore one another altogether. The first of the two moronic men stubbornly sat back down and pushed back as far as he could, crossed his arms and feigned sleeping. The other just covered himself up quietly in his blanket, looking at me with a forlorn attitude. Just like two insolent children.

I was doing the job I'd be trained to do. Hopefully this trip wouldn't test me with any more crazy situations. But I was prepared for whatever might happen.

Seventeen

THE END OF THE SUPER COMMUTE

"There's no way we'll make it, unless we go up to Philly tomorrow," John said. Here we go again, giving up more time off. How I hated that. The commute from Ft. Lauderdale was getting tougher. A new cruise terminal had recently opened, so the cruisers flew in and out, filling seats and making it difficult for those of us attempting to fly on standby.

"So I guess I'm going to have to tell the sitter that we're not leaving Sunday, but Saturday instead, and she'd have to babysit Pamela an extra day," I said disdainfully. "This is getting old." I felt victimized. I missed driving to Miami International to start my trips. These last minute changes were nerve wracking. I hated leaving Pamela any more that I had to.

But our newly merged airline executives had decided that the Miami base was unprofitable, and concentrated on growing hubs up north instead.

We resisted moving to a base hub. Pamela was only six and her father lived nearby. Our divorce, the sale of her childhood home, and new marriage was enough of a change for her in just a matter of two years. She had friends and family to look forward to being with when I was flying. We liked living in the warm climate in South Florida.

Flying the day before a trip meant paying for hotels. And of course, extra time away from home without any extra compensation. I tried to bid a schedule that departed late so that I could fly up the same day of starting work.

Bidding my schedule was a chore as I'd have to check each trip very closely. I wanted the ones with a late departure and that finished early.

"Try to avoid commuting on cruise day," said a co-worker. "The ships come in and sometimes they arrive early so the cruisers try to get on the earlier flights—bumping people like us." Standby. Loved it and hated it. Flying for free was a nice perk, but one could never depend on getting a seat.

Even the best of planning didn't always work. Mondays was when most business people flew. Tuesdays were ideal, but I wasn't always lucky enough to get Tuesday trips.

I gave myself weekly pep talks. But sometimes I'd have nightmares about commuting. I'd dream about getting in trouble. Not being able to make it to work as a result of being bumped was a bad mark in my otherwise impeccable record.

We packed and left early on Saturday afternoon. I felt guilty leaving Pamela. It was happening more and more often. But if it bothered her, she didn't tell me. She seemed happy to see Patty, the sitter. But I missed her a lot, especially when I had to leave sooner than planned.

As I settled back in my seat on the flight to Philadelphia, John put his hand on my knee. I felt that he sensed my displeasure about leaving home sooner than planned. He didn't seem happy about it either.

Once we landed, we made the best of our situation, checked into the airport hotel, and went out for dinner. We talked about our trip the next day, and our layover cities. Boston. Orlando. San Diego. Boston was the long overnight and we planned on visiting the city and enjoying some good fish at Legal Seafood. Boston had different fish than we were used to in the south. The stay in Orlando would be a short one with a late arrival and early departure, just enough time to sleep before flying again. We'd have a long stay in San Diego and I looked forward to the Seaport Village on the bay. That was a fun place to jog in the morning then sit at a café for coffee and breakfast. There was an old bookstore that I liked to browse, which was part of the coffee shop.

I called Pamela later that night and 'tucked her in bed' from Philadelphia. I made calls to her on a daily basis after she'd get home from school. In the late 1980's cell phone use was for elite executives, and no flight attendant or pilot had the mobile devices that are now the norm. I knew where every pay phone was at the airport. They were my lifeline. On rare occasions, she'd cry and ask me when I'd be back. But most of the time she was a happy little girl who'd share her latest accomplishments with joy.

"Mommy, guess what? I got to be the teacher's helper today!" She'd exclaim.

We had a four-day and would be back Wednesday, God willing, if the flights home weren't full. So far they looked promising—plenty of open seats.

⌒

*W*e met our crew the next day. John and I had a pact between us—we'd first check with each other before inviting anyone to go out with us on the overnights. There were some people we'd just as soon not socialize with, and others whom we wanted to get to know better. During a break in between flights, we'd talk it over. The conversation would go, "I like this crew. Let's invite them to go out—what do you think?" or "I think I'd rather just be the two of us…" Sometimes a day of flying was tiring enough to warrant room service. We relied on intuition and usually felt the same way, which made the two of us compatible and willing to fly together all the time.

On this particular four-day, the crew acted like one big happy family.

"Where do you commute from?" was the usual icebreaker. The assumption seemed to be that no one lived in a base city. But with so many changes that were common in the airline industry, many pilots' and flight attendants' home bases had been closed. This airline was no exception. We'd gone from having seven bases to three. It was called "right-sizing" a catchphrase for downsizing and being more efficient and thus more profitable.

I was interested in knowing where others resided.

"I live in Norfolk," said one.

"I commute from Greensboro."

"I live in New York."

The co-pilot lived in Sacramento. "It's a choice. I live where I want to live," he said. Indeed. I loved Florida and never wanted to live anywhere else. I'd travelled the world all my life and Ft. Lauderdale felt like home to me.

All of us commuted. Our highways to work were the airways in the skies on standby which made it difficult. It was our responsibility either to move to a base, or deal with the consequences. Checking and re-checking flight loads were a normal routine for commuting flight crewmembers.

The crew went out to dinner together in Boston where I savored a baked scrod and Chardonnay. Ah, the perks of the job, flying around the country and going out to dinner in a different city. We spoke about our commuting adventures.

"I barely made it this morning. The flight from Norfolk showed plenty of open seats—until the one before it cancelled. So they filled up the one I was on, but thank God there were still a couple of seats left," said Ellie.

"That happened to me last week. I *didn't* make it and I'm in trouble," said Dave the New Yorker. "I'm on level three dependability." I shuddered at the thought of being in the dependability program. Flight attendants were on constant monitoring by the bosses in the dependability program and more commuting problems could result in termination. I'd been lucky. So far no problems. But would my luck continue?

We talked about our families, but the conversation reverted back to our commutes and the drama surrounding that. People love drama, I thought. I relayed a story of my own about a trip that finished late. I had barely enough time to catch my flight home. As soon as the last passenger had deplaned, I jumped off and jogged in my high heels from one terminal to another. I got to the gate, out of breath and ran through the jet way to the plane as fast as I could. The agent was closing the aircraft door.

"Any seats left?" I asked, out of breath. Sweat was pouring down my face and inside my blouse.

"No, sorry," the agent said, "it's full."

"What about the jump seat?" I asked. There was usually at least one spare jump seat available that we could ride while in uniform.

"Another commuting flight attendant took it. Sorry."

She didn't seem like she was sorry. My heart sank. It was the last flight out. I'd have to wait until morning. I found a hotel near the airport and sank into the bed longing for my own after four days of being away.

Scenarios like these became more and more typical as flights got fuller with each drop in ticket price that made flying more affordable.

"I sure wish they'd increase the number of flights or something," Ellie said.

"I wish they'd open up a Ft. Lauderdale or Miami base again," I said wishfully.

As the end of our trip approached, we were happy because we'd arrived in plenty of time to catch an early flight and get home before dark—an unusual blessing. Most of the time we'd have to take late flights and get home with barely enough time to fix a quick dinner before collapsing in bed. I'd feel so exhausted the next morning when I'd get up at six to make breakfast and take Pamela to school.

This time would be different. We relished the idea of enjoying some day-light once we got home. Maybe we could sit out on the patio before bedtime. Pamela could share her stories with us. We'd have a little wine and some dinner before turning in—that would be nice. We settled into our seats and I closed my eyes for a quick catnap, feeling lucky to have this unusual early commute back to Ft. Lauderdale.

"Ladies and Gentlemen, this is your captain speaking. We're going to have a delay here in Philadelphia due to a hydraulic problem. The mechanics will be assessing the situation for us and I will let you know when we can expect to depart." *Oh no.*

John looked at me shaking his head. I sank back into my seat and closed my eyes again. Maybe it would get fixed soon. It'll be okay.

Awhile later the captain informed us it would be one and a half hours. But even with this delay we'd still be home earlier than usual.

"It won't be bad," I said to John.

An hour after we took off, we heard the captain tell us we'd have to make an unscheduled stop in Charlotte. The hydraulic problem persisted and needed serious attention. The leak hadn't been fixed properly.

When we landed in Charlotte the flight was cancelled. Passengers were rerouted which meant no seats for us poor standbys. We looked for other ways to get home with the help of a compassionate agent. She was very creative, but it took an hour to figure out what we had to do. She routed us on an open flight back north to Pittsburgh. From PIT, we'd get on the last flight to Ft. Lauderdale. That flight was open too. We'd be home by one in the morning. I had to call the sitter to keep Pamela one more night because of our dilemma—well laid out plans gone awry.

Bedraggled, we got home and went right to bed. But John and I were feeling anxious and couldn't sleep right away. I broke the silence as we sat in bed, unable to fall asleep. John was channel surfing the TV.

"I think we've got to move," I said. "This is too much. We're spending too much of our time commuting. And this was exhausting—a drain of our precious energy."

"Are you serious?" he said. "Do you know what that entails? You *do* know that means selling the house, leaving your family and uprooting Pamela?"

"But a move close to Philly would make life much easier," I said. "It might be fun. Change of seasons. New territory. And *driving to work.*"

"Once we start the process, there's no looking back," said John.

"Let's do it," I said.

Three months later we found a house and moved to Wilmington, Delaware, twenty minutes south of the PHL International Airport. It was the biggest house I'd ever had. A beautiful brownstone in a small subdivision called Country Gates, with a pool and a large fenced backyard full of tall trees. I looked forward to our new life ahead.

Eighteen

PARISIAN FEASTS AND A ROSARY FROM ROME

We hadn't realized that the season for using the swimming pool in Delaware would only last two or three months at the max. Fall arrived in late August as the sunlight turned hazy and more distant and cooler days set in. The beautiful trees surrounding the pool shed all their leaves rendering them completely bare. Thankfully we'd learned the pool had to be covered before that happened. Raking the leaves in the brisk autumn weather was invigorating—but not one of our favorite things to do.

The furnishings we'd brought with us from our small house in Florida barely filled the five-bedroom one. But I wasn't in a hurry to fill empty spaces. I wanted to get a feeling first for what we needed. Styles were different up north. Décor was more traditional and wood pieces darker than what I'd been used to. In time I trusted that I'd find the right things.

I hoped we'd get some snow. I hadn't lived in cold weather since my days as a child in Paris. Maybe we'd go sledding at a nearby state park.

"We had a terrible winter last year," said a neighbor. "Hopefully it won't happen again for awhile. The roads get icy and dangerous." I hadn't thought of that. How bad could it be?

Flying became much easier. No more super-commuting wasting time and leaving Pamela more days than was necessary.

We found a family who had a daughter Pamela's age and she stayed with them during our trips. John and I didn't fly together and flew opposite days so that we could be home to help Pamela with the transition. After awhile when we did get to fly together, we decided it was more conducive to have someone stay at the house so that she wouldn't have to pack every week like we did. That would give her more stability.

Soon after our move I began flying Internationally. There was a need for French and Italian language speakers and I was ready for a new chapter in my career. I was excited to go back to Europe to visit the places I'd once lived. I hoped that we'd fly to Greece someday. I missed my mother. Annual two-week visits just didn't satisfy my needs and I wanted to see her more often.

I had to pass the language fluency tests to qualify as a LODO flight attendant. LODO is the acronym for a flight attendant qualified in the Language of Destination or Origin. USAir arranged for me to go to Berlitz to be tested in French and Italian conversation. It wasn't easy. There were technical words—not everyday language— pertaining to aircraft and flying that I had to learn. The first part of the ninety-minute session was conversational with the second half consisting of structured questions and answers pertaining to travel and airplane stuff. I passed both languages with high grades. I couldn't wait to start the trips.

It took me awhile to get used to working long flights. The longest flights I'd ever worked up until then were coast to coast in the U.S. Paris was over seven hours and my legs and feet hurt by the time we landed. I was tired flying during the night. There were designated crew rest seats that were curtained off for quiet time, sleep or just relaxing with a book to read. Crews took turns being on duty. But I looked forward to a real bed when we landed.

The hotel in Montparnasse, a suburb of Paris, was fancy compared to the ones we stayed in the U.S. We'd arrive in the early morning. I could smell delicious fresh croissants in the lobby that came from the dimly lit dining room. French coffee. *Mmmmm.* But first I needed sleep.

Crews typically napped about four hours and then forced themselves to wake up. The way I was feeling it would have been easy to sleep the day away but that would leave no time to get out and explore the city. Departure was the following day; our stay was scheduled for twenty-six hours. I'd get a good eight hours of sleep before the next day's departure.

I took the metro to the old school and our old house. I chose Paris initially so that I could find my old neighborhood—and the school where I was out of my comfort zone, bullied and forced to learn French at the age of seven. When I found it, I stood outside and said "merci" out loud to the old white building. Had it not been for that period in my life I would have not had the 'super seniority' to fly to Paris. Memories flooded me and I felt a twinge in my stomach as I reminisced about my younger years. The innocence as children at play with my sister and brother. Our beautiful home. My mother's and father's nurturing. The kids jeering at me when I couldn't understand them. The one friend I'd made, a caring tutor who brought me up to language proficiency. I couldn't wait to tell my mom about seeing our old dwelling. Paris was one of her favorite places to live.

The crews loved going to eat at a bistro in Breteuille, a suburb near Montparnasse. I often went for dinner with them and enjoyed a four-course meal of boeuf bourguignon or seafood crepes, with a starter of escargots. Dessert was crème brulee. French wine. After a few of those dining experiences my uniform began to feel tight. Thankfully the weight standards that were so strict had been relaxed to more realistic numbers, but I was determined not to order a larger size uniform. I decided I'd exercise and eat more healthfully.

Other Paris layovers varied from shopping at a favorite culinary kitchen store on Rue de Rennes and roaming the Galleries La Fayette to look at fashions I couldn't afford. France was very expensive. The Champs Elysees, famous in postcard pictures and movies, was one of my favorite streets to walk, losing a few extra pounds of weight along the way.

*I*t was convenient to drive home after finishing a trip in Philadelphia. No more stand-by flying home. But I still missed Ft. Lauderdale.

But Pamela didn't adjust as well. I began to feel guilty for bringing her north and leaving my brother and sister—her aunt and uncle, and her friends and the school that she loved. I felt victimized. But I kept rationalizing that I'd lived like that all my life— moving around, and that it had been a valuable experience. There were lessons in resilience and cultural differences. Still, she didn't buy into it as easily as I thought. Her resilience towards change had come to an end.

"Just think, soon we'll get some snow—we can go sledding in Brandywine Creek Park," I said. She'd shrug her shoulders, seemingly disconnected. I became concerned and we went for family counseling where she didn't say much. The counselor wrote it off as a typical transition into adolescence.

The fall weather was beautiful. We'd never experienced such a kaleidoscope of colors in Florida. Leaves turned orange, red, yellow and we relished taking drives through the winding hilly roads in the Brandywine Valley to take it all in. The Brandywine River sparkled as a backdrop, its color a bright cerulean blue and silver with reflections of puffy clouds and sunlight.

I'd turned one of the rooms in the house into a studio and began painting. I wanted to capture those fall scenes in watercolor on paper. For every good painting I must have thrown away ten. But I didn't let that stop me. It took practice. Someday I'd spend more time doing it as I wanted to get better. There was something about creating a work of art, the process seemed to make time stand still. It gave me great peace and joy.

We encouraged Pamela to get involved with sports or any activities she might think of. Volleyball became her passion for a short while and we were relieved that she'd found an outlet. She befriended her teammates. There were tournaments to participate in. We went on many road trips to Penn State University and Maryland. We flew to Florida State in Tallahassee for volleyball camp.

But all was not well. I missed Florida. Pamela and I began to have mother-daughter spats. I became depressed and that didn't help.

"That's normal. She's preteen and it might even escalate sometimes," another parent told me.

I wondered what happened to my little girl and why she wasn't happy. She rarely wanted to talk. Her grades were below average. Was my flying career in the way of a good mother- daughter relationship? Blaming my career became the easy thing to do. If I hadn't become a flight attendant...That was it. If we hadn't left Florida...

"Maybe she's angry you moved," said Tisha whom I continued to confide in.

Cold weather set in and the first few snows were fun. That was the rare occasion

Pamela would join us for sledding down steep hills and my heart soared happily when I'd see her laugh with glee as she'd glide down the slopes.

I became bored flying to Paris after a year and switched to a schedule of Rome trips as soon as there was a vacancy.

Rome was a walking town like Paris. I enjoyed long afternoons exploring the city. At times I'd make the long walk from the Via Veneto area to the Vatican, passing the Piazza di Spagna and walking the crowded streets making a detour to see the Pantheon. Nearby would be Trevi Fountain which looked surreal with its beautiful sculptures and flowing waters. Scooters whizzed by. Along the way, I'd stop at Piazza Navonna and people-watch while sipping on a glass of wine. I liked this Piazza with its artists proudly displaying their work. I bought a small painting there to remind me of Roma.

I visited our old apartment. My Catholic school where I grew to love the nuns who were my teachers. I was glad my Papa didn't want me to become a nun. How smart of him—my life was much richer even with the upheavals, divorces, moves and remarriages.

Was there a life without upheaval? I longed for happiness. What would it take?

The culinary tastes of Italy, like France, were a distraction. I enjoyed many a pizza and lots of pasta in all shapes. Roasted veal. Chicken Marsala platters. Spinach sprinkled with fresh Parmegiano Regianno and pine nuts drenched in olive oil topped with fried bits of fresh bacon. I became fearful of being overtaken by my love of eating. I understood the notion that 'Europeans live to eat while Americans eat to live.'

I took up running. It made me feel better emotionally while doing its job to keep me trim. I did a lot of thinking and self pep-talking during those runs in the park. Things would get better. She'd outgrow her rebellion soon.

But things at home got tense and I had a nagging suspicion they weren't going to improve. Thankfully John was a pillar of strength and the voice of reason whenever I'd let my temper flare up—which was often as I let my frustrations get the best of me

I went to work with a heavy heart. Sure, it was nice *driving* to work. But at what cost now? I wondered what to do next and kept blaming my career.

"I hate your job," Pamela screamed to me one day. Was she validating my suspicion or simply pushing a sensitive button? I'd heard that before from her father.

One day I told John, "I want to quit flying."

"Maybe you can take a leave of absence. I think you'd regret it if you quit," he said. But I'd reached a point where even the International flying wasn't pleasant. I kept focusing on the strife at home.

On a flight from Rome one afternoon, a nun stopped me in the aisle. I knelt next to her to listen as she spoke to me in a low soft voice. Handing me a rosary, she said, "Take this. I see sorrow in your eyes—I can feel it. Mother Mary will listen to your prayers. You will not endure this pain forever. Trust in God. Things will get better. Pray."

I thanked her as tears welled up in my eyes and put it in my pocket. Although I am not Catholic or religious, I did pray, asking for answers and peace.

The Rosary still sits on my nightstand to this day.

MY PARENTS, ROSE AND RONNIE ON THEIR WEDDING DAY IN 1945

THE PLANE RIDE FROM TOKYO TO ATHENS. A LOCKHEED
CONSTELLATION, WHERE I GOT THE CALLING.

THE ENTICING BROCHURE.

GRADUATION DAY. 1984. CEO OF EASTERN FRANK BORMAN
PINNED MY WINGS THAT DAY.

Two special guests at graduation. My sister Pam and daughter Pamela

FLYING "EL INTERAMERICANO" SERVICE TO SOUTH AMERICA.

My friend Tisha and me flying together and a having
a photo op on the wing of a DC9 at USAir.

Meeting John in 1990.

CHRISTMAS CARD PHOTO-OP 1994, WITH PAMELA.

FLYING WITH CAPTAIN JOHN.

WITH MY FRIEND REZA, TWO GREEK AND FRENCH SPEAKING LODO'S.

Nineteen

WAKING UP

I was feeling uneasy and confused in the freezing cold air-conditioned room. Was I the only one? I looked around and saw other forlorn-looking parents like myself, some of them putting on their sweaters. I shivered. I'm not alone. People seated around me appeared to be having the same malaise I was experiencing. My stomach churned. Oh God, please let these three days be good. Noticing my angst, John put his hand on my leg, in his way of silently reassuring me that everything was going to be okay. But I sensed that he too, was anxious. The room was silent as we awaited the seminar to begin.

The most difficult thing we had ever done was behind us. Just a few weeks ago, after much research, we'd finally made the decision to do what we'd been avoiding for a while. We'd placed Pamela into a boarding school. We hadn't spoken to each other since then, four months— what seemed like an eternity. This was the rule, we were told. I missed her. But we were relieved knowing that she was safe.

"Your child needs time to herself. You will not be able to talk until she reaches Level Three. Meanwhile we recommend that you attend "Discovery" seminar," said the parent-child counselor. "Discovery is the first of three, the next one will be held in Seattle—unless you want to wait a few more months when it will be held on the east coast." We had passes to fly so we signed up for the cross-country trip having decided to get started sooner. And there we were, clueless about what was to come next.

There'd been other options. Military schools, Catholic boarding schools. But this seemed to be the best choice, highly recommended by a pilot friend.

Our view of the facility that we placed Pam in had a system that generated a positive peer-pressure focusing on choices and results. Desirable results brought rewards. There was a level system. All of the teens started at Level One and earned points to make it to the next levels. Upper levels were comprised of teens who'd been at the school for several months, had undergone training and mastered accountability. They were the role models. The lower level kids looked up to their higher-level peers, vying to become leaders someday too—a worthy goal to aim for. As in the game of life itself, good deeds and hard work paved the way to more privileges. One such privilege was being allowed to speak to mom and dad in a weekly phone call. Rules were regimented with a strict routine consisting of academics and housekeeping. The students had to attend seminars like the one we were in. Pamela had already been through "Discovery".

We'd lied to her the day we took her to the school, telling her that we were going on a little impromptu vacation, just the three of us. I felt guilty. But had we told her what we were up to, I was afraid she'd run away. I cringed at the thought; her running away was a constant fear. The kids she was hanging out with scared me. I couldn't force my sixteen year old to stay away from them. I had lost control.

Had I met the teenager that I once was? I was not so naïve as not to realize kids like to experiment.

Her sweetness had vanished. Her smiles and laughter were replaced by darkness and anger. I no longer knew the child that was part of our family. What happened? My baby girl had lost her innocence and we needed to do something to save her, and our sanity.

Arranging for the trip was easy. She didn't resist like I assumed she would. Did I did see a glimmer of light when I told her we were going for a little vacation? Excitement? Maybe there was hope after all. Maybe she thought we were going on one of those white water rafting trips again. Camping and hiking. I missed doing things together as a family. Trips to Greece. Disney World vacations in Ft. Wilderness with campfire sing-alongs. Those days had long passed.

We used our free passes to fly to South Carolina. I thanked God for my job that offered this perk since we were in the throes of sudden decision-making. Last minute airline tickets would have cost a fortune. I fought back tears as John drove the rental car up and down the hilly country roads on our way to a little town called Due West, SC. Pamela sat in the back seat, oblivious. She wore her headset, listening to a cassette tape player. I could tell it was music. Explicit rap. I had given up the battle over her music choices a long time ago. There were battles over everything from clothes to curfews.

Now at the Discovery seminar, my mind ruminated about the day we left her at school. Did we do the right thing? What if she hated me for the rest of her life? Where did I go wrong? Maybe if I had been a stay-at-home mom... Maybe if I hadn't divorced her father...Maybe if I worked a day job instead of flying...Maybe-maybe-maybe. These questions haunted me day after day. Beating myself up emotionally became a habit. I was a victim, wracked with doubt. What could we have done differently? I felt pangs of guilt. The land of guilt became my hangout of choice.

When we got to the facility, I handed her over to the intake woman. I told her she had to stay there for a while and kissed her goodbye.

Four months had passed since then.

⟨⟩

My reverie was interrupted when a facilitator by the name of Duane entered the room, and stood front and center. He was well over six feet tall, a good-looking black man in good shape with a powerful stance. He wore a pin stripe suit, tie and a crisp white shirt. With a sincere and engaging manner he swept us quickly into rapt attention.

"Welcome to Discovery, ladies and gentlemen. (*pause*). You are here because there has been a serious disruption in your lives. (*long pause*). What's at stake here? Your quality of life. Your home and the people you love."

No kidding.

Then he asked us a rhetorical question, "What happened before you got here?" He had a booming voice.

I had just been thinking about that. Where was he going with this?

"Each and every one of you has something in common—family. There has been war in your home, and your house has become a battlefield..."

I was mesmerized. I looked around the room. John was squeezing my knee hard as he listened. We glanced at each other tentatively. I was grateful to have him sitting next to me.

The walls in the seminar room were lined with posters containing strange messages. The first one read, *"That which is not acted upon is not learned."* Another read, *"What I fear, I create."* And, *"Nothing can change when you are comfortable."* Reading the posters made me feel confused. I sensed that we were in for an eye-opening ride. I would stick through this to the end. For Pamela.

Little did I know—it was not for Pamela. It was for me.

As the day progressed, things got more difficult. We were told not to sit next to the same person after each break. There were confrontational encounters. I began to realize that this was a place where the ego would be challenged and "mirrors" would be coming up for us to take a hard look at ourselves, our belief systems and our family dynamics.

That afternoon we were put into groups and asked to give feedback to one another based on our gut feelings and experiences of each other. There was to be no sugar-coating. And no responding. Simply delivering feedback and receiving it from others when it was our turn. I felt an enormous heaviness in my heart. I wanted to bolt out of the room. Was this what the kids were doing too?

We were to begin our feedback by telling the recipient, "My experience of you is..." or "What I feel when I am around you is..."

What I heard from my peers was painful.

"You're worn out."

"You act like you're unhappy and beat down."

"Sad-sack mom."

Duh—that *was me*.

"You think you're perfect."

"You're unapproachable." Big eye opener. I knew I'd failed to connect—really connect, with Pamela anymore.

I was thrown into feeling vulnerable. I cried. The discomfort led me to the poster on the wall that read, *"Nothing is Learned When You Are Comfortable."* What would I learn today?

I needed to change my thinking and to stop hanging out in the land of guilt—my familiar place of refuge.

We were not allowed to leave the room except during infrequent breaks. One man who'd lost his patience vehemently shouted at Duane:

"I travelled hundreds of miles to this mandatory piece of shit seminar and I'm *not* going to be told I can't leave the room and have a cigarette."

"Stop. I want you to stop and take a look at your behavior, sir. And your smoking habit. Is it a son or a daughter in school?" Duane asked.

"Son! And this is all bullshit!" "Aha. Have you seen this type of behavior in him perhaps?" The man went storming out of the room. A verbal illustration ensued about how the way we acted in the room served as a mirror that illustrated how we acted and reacted in day-to-day life. The man had dropped out of the seminar. I felt sorry for his family, especially his son in the program. All that for a cigarette break!

There was a module about "blame." How quick we are to blame. Duane related a story about blasting a gate agent regarding a delayed flight. Common behavior? I'd seen it a few times in my career. Passengers blaming flight attendants when they didn't like their seat assignment, or if we didn't have their favorite beverage. There was an illustration about our role modeling for the younger generations.

There was a module about setting clear intentions. *"Based on your results you have what you intended."* Another lecture was about the ways we "avoid." I remembered using my flying to avoid dealing with a failing marriage. And worse, the denial that ensued when I blamed my marital issues on my ex, even though I thought I'd tried my best. I had "checked out" of that marriage with the affair.

Oh brother. Let this be over. The digging felt like being in a gigantic mud puddle. Cold. Dirty. The first day lasted sixteen hours, ending with a failed team-building exercise. Instead of working together, we competed against one another. We hadn't paid attention to the rules of the game. Learning. Learning. Learning.

We barely had five hours of sleep before returning for what John called 'cruel punishment'. Nevertheless, we stuck through it. Tolerant. Curious. Tired. What would tomorrow bring?

Day two was no easier. A dark room. Reflecting upon our own moms and dads. What was left unsaid. Had I made peace with my mom? We'd avoided talking about our issues. I'd do that as soon as I could. I loved her and wanted to hold her close to me, tell her I was sorry for the hurtful things I'd done. I found myself wanting to express the immense gratitude for my life borne by her and Papa who had passed on years earlier from lung cancer. I felt them close to me, grateful for the parents that I had, and had often taken for granted.

There were lectures on Perfection versus Excellence. I always strived to be perfect. Often frustrated if things weren't always perfect, no doubt influencing Pamela over recent times with undesirable outcomes.

"Striving for perfection usually leads to disappointment. Perfection is an illusion. How about being *excellent* instead?" What is "perfect" anyway?

The last day was one of reflective expression. We were asked to share our experiences and what we'd learned. There were great revelations made by parents like me. Duane's effective facilitation impacted me in positive ways. I entertained the idea that I might like to be a teacher like him someday, to help other people and be a conduit for them to realize their best and highest potential ways of being.

There were more seminars to sign up for.

At closing we were formed into small groups to perform impromptu singing skits, being reminded by Duane "resistance now was futile." We had fun and it was a magical time watching grown adults singing, dancing, acting like gleeful kids. I'd forgotten what that felt like—letting myself go and being in the moment of play. My introverted husband John winced at having to 'perform' his skit. He said he did it for Pam, but we both knew he learned a lot about himself too in the process.

I had divested myself of the victim that resided in me. I was now convinced we'd done the right thing. I felt the freedom to fly in my life and at work. Guilt free.

Before heading back east, we spent the next day sightseeing in Seattle and getting a seafood fix at Pike's Place Market. After the long days in a confined atmosphere it was a good reprieve and reconnection as a couple, sharing our thoughts as we strolled in the city and admired the beautiful flowers that adorned the market. We went to the Space Needle where the view of the city was breathtaking. I had a delicious halibut dinner that evening and savored some Chardonnay since we hadn't been allowed any alcohol as part of the ground rules during the three days.

The flight home was uneventful. I dreaded once again going into an empty house knowing that I wasn't going to see my Pamela. I knew the time would come, but when?

She had joined the school chorus, having earned the privilege to sing with her group at a local assisted-living home for the elderly. We had weekly reports over the phone and things seemed to be going well.

And then a surprise came.

"Mary I am happy to tell you that Pamela made Level Three. We're very proud of her and she would like to talk to you." My heart skipped a few beats. That's my girl!

"Oh yes, that would be great!" was all I could muster. After a long pause I heard the voice of an upbeat young lady.

"Mom, I just want to tell you I love you so much. Thanks for doing Discovery seminar, it means a lot to me. Some parents don't, or if they do they don't make it all the way through...and oh yes, did they tell you I am in a chorus. Can I sing you a song?"

"Yes!"

With that, she belted out a verse to the lyrics to *"Wind Beneath My Wings"* by Beth Midler.

"It might have appeared to go unnoticed
But I have you right here in my heart. I want you to know,
I know the truth of course.
That I would be nothing without you.
Did you ever know that you're my hero?
You're everything I would like to be.
I can fly higher than eagle.
And you are the wind beneath my wings."

My heart soared like it never had on any airplane, ever. I cried tears of joy. Nothing else mattered. Pam was finding herself and so was I. And in the process I'd have my family back.

But there'd be much more work for us still to do. I was ready.

Twenty

GETTING FOCUSED

I flew back to Seattle for the second seminar, again with free passes for air travel. I still marveled that I could use passes for this. Not just for a commute to work or for vacation travel, but also for workshops and seminars that were held in all parts of the country.

My next seminar was called *"Focus"*. It would last four days. It was led by a lady named Lou. An incredible woman with piercing blue eyes and a raspy voice, she challenged us further down the road that Duane had paved for us. Just when I thought I'd learned new skills, there were more lessons in store. The same posters as before adorned the walls: *'That which is not acted upon is not learned.'* and *'Nothing changes when we are comfortable.'*

Here we go again. I began shifting in my seat the minute Ms. Lou began to speak. A challenging voice with rhetorical questions, she spoke about accountability and how we ended up here in the room. Pamela had also attended Focus by this time. My mind wandered as I thought about how she might have fared. I caught myself and stopped, realizing that I needed to stay in the present. It was new learning for me as I caught myself projecting onto Pamela instead of focusing on myself. It happened on the plane when I worked, or at home while she was away. The worried mother. Flying had gotten easier without the grief of worrying if she was in danger, or what I'd find when I'd return back home. But I still worried. Would I be a good mom if I didn't worry?

"Let her work on herself. You do your work," I was told.

There were modules in feedback that went deeper than before.

"You are too perfect, or try to be," I heard. Ouch.

"You're a taker—you have sorrow about your family's situation written all over your face and it's all you talk about—how much you worry..." Ouch twice. I wanted to be a giver not a taker. I was jealous of the 'givers' in the room. They participated more and exuded a certain kind of passion and leadership about them that I'd lost somewhere.

We were given performing assignments to do the last day. Mine was to dress, sing and dance as Shania Twain in front of seventy participant parents. To the song, *"Man I Feel Like a Woman."*

I didn't know why I got this as my 'stretch' performance act. Until it dawned on me later that I had shown up stiff and uptight with my buttoned-to-the-chin blouses. I listened to the song for the underlying theme. I liked it. It moved me and I thought I could do this.

We were given some time to come up with our costumes. There was a mall across the street where I bought a cowboy hat, an oversized white blouse and a short skirt (perfect for the part of the song that says "Man's shirts, shorts skirts...") I had to get my sexy back. Had I gotten so caught up in being Ms. Worry Mom that I'd forgotten how?

I was scared and didn't sleep the night before. My perfection issues crept up on me and the fear of failing, or being judged in front of my peers. All this consumed me in nightmares. Was I alone? We were all in the same situation. Maybe that was the whole point—to stretch beyond our comfort zones and overcome the need to stay "safe". There was a lot of overcoming to be done. I felt as if I was just about to jump off a cliff.

The jump became a blast of a party. I witnessed other parents coming out of their shells. The creative costumes were out-of-this-world fabulous. One woman went from being a cocoon to a butterfly with colorful paper mache and silk scarves. A man who had been overly talkative was given the assignment to be a mime and relay a message without speaking.

As I danced and sang my song with abandon, I felt alive once again. Unafraid of what others were thinking. The air was magic. I felt like a child again basking in that freedom that is like flying. How do we lose that?

It was the breakthrough I needed, much like the feeling I had when I spoke in the flight attendant interview room so successfully at last. Children experiment outside of their comfort zones. When does that change? It changes when harsh judgment overtakes encouragement.

John and I had stopped having fun together by being consumed and distraught with Pamela. Thankfully the strength of our love prevailed throughout that time period. I'd become jaded with people and my job. But I transformed into a much happier person on the plane. The self-absorption was killing me before and looking back, I fail to recognize the person that I was. I was no longer the forlorn mother feeling beaten down by outside influences, throwing her arms up in the air in frustration.

I learned that choice was a beautiful thing we possessed. When did I forget that? How powerful is it that we can respond without going into emotional reactive states? How wonderful it was to practice analyzing my anger, fears and cynicism—all part of the human condition—and moving on…

My relationship with Pamela was good after she returned from the program school. She thanked us for 'saving her life'. I thanked her for the lessons too. She wasn't the perfect child who followed the agenda that we had planned for her. She had her own ideas and exuded independence that was difficult for me to handle at times, but I chose to let things go. When I disagreed with her I made sure it was about a choice and not her persona. It wasn't about choosing battles. There was no need for battling. We could communicate.

Today my beloved daughter and I have an excellent honest and open relationship. I shared my guilt about leaving her, being a flight attendant.

"Oh Mom, I was always so proud of you. I'm glad you have a job that makes you happy," she said.

Flying became easier without the burdens of letting events consume me, thus giving up my power to them. I'd grown to neutralize situations that would otherwise charge me up with anger or frustration.

I still had lots more to learn and was ready to take on the challenges. Flying for free was a perk that helped me travel to many places to attend more seminars and workshops. The next ones were designed for me to explore my many interests. There were so many passions. Art classes. Volunteering to assist the seminar facilitators like Lou and Duane. Becoming a facilitator and teacher. Writing.

Flying was fulfilling, but it was no longer enough. I wanted to do more.

There were classes being offered to certify as a Life Coach. And another to learn seminar facilitation. Art workshops. An abundant cornucopia awaited me.

Pamela would be coming home soon. I was excited.

Twenty-One

THE DAY I'LL NEVER FORGET

*C*olors began to change. It was a crisp fall morning with periwinkle blue skies and a chill in the air. The leaves were still green in Delaware, but they were bright and translucent in the sunlight. I liked the fall season, but didn't look forward to winter. I didn't like the cold but I liked sweater-weather.

The longer we lived up north, the more I missed and longed for Florida. Would we ever move back? Perhaps when we retired someday.

I was standing in front of the bathroom mirror putting on my make-up getting ready to work a trip to Rome that afternoon. I'd told John I wanted to take a leave from flying, but the airline wasn't offering any time off. I was close to quitting because my job seemed to get in the way of other things I'd rather be doing.

As I finished drying my hair, John came in from his office and said, "Hey, Sheika come here, there's something weird going on." He'd just gotten a call from a friend telling him to turn onto the news channel.

I put down my hairbrush and joined him where he was standing in front of the bedroom TV that was delivering a breaking story. We stood together as we watched it unfold, mesmerized and in shock.

"It looks like a plane had an accident and ran into one of the Twin Towers." John said.

"That's horrible!" I said, wondering what could have gone wrong.

There were a couple of replays of the event. But after fifteen minutes, it was not a replay. There was another plane that the cameras captured as it slammed into the second tower rendering it into flames. The scene played out live in front of our eyes at the moment of impact.

"That was another one! That wasn't an accident!" John said as we watched the second strike into the other tower, live. I got goose bumps. My legs trembled. My stomach lurched. What was going on?

We looked at each other, bewildered. From that moment, we were glued to the news that was unfolding in front of our eyes. New York City was in chaos. There were scenes of people fleeing the falling debris. The air looked like a thick gray veil.

It was obvious that we were under attack, but very little information was forthcoming as to by whom and why. Much later it was revealed that a terrorist group known as Al Qaida had hijacked airliners, murdering innocent victims to make their case against the United States and the world at large. Airplanes still loaded with fuel became missiles. I couldn't imagine the terror in the Twin Tower buildings or the airplanes.

There were two more planes that were hijacked. One crashed into the ground near Pittsburgh and another flew into the Pentagon. When would this end?

Bridges were closed going in and out of Manhattan. President George W. Bush, who'd been visiting and reading to children at a Florida public school was alerted and flown back to Washington. Airports were shut down and planes grounded after being diverted to the nearest airports. Flight crews and passengers were stranded for up to four or more days until flights resumed again.

Schools closed, sending children home. I met Pamela as she walked to the house, her face ashen. Both of us were in shock.

"Mom—what happened?" she asked. I didn't know what to say. I was just relieved to have my daughter walking next to me, safe. We were finally a family united together after her stint in South Carolina. It was her senior year.

"I'm just glad we're all okay. It looks like there's been a terrorist attack," was all I could muster. We walked home in silence.

"I don't think you're flying tonight, honey," John said. Dispatch had called to say my flight had cancelled.

I was relieved, having dreaded getting on a plane after the morning's events. Fear had overtaken our family and our nation. Our house was on a direct flight path to Philadelphia airport and the skies had become eerily silent.

Neighbors gathered. There were questions to John asking for his pilot's perspective. As if surely he'd have some inside scoop. We'd been trained to intervene in hijackings as best we could. It seemed the crews this time were taken completely off guard. Little did we know the effect this would have on life in the free world. The events of that day changed the face of commercial aviation, as we knew it.

I wondered about inbound flights from Europe. Some were diverted back to European cities, if they were still close enough. But the ones that were already in flight halfway across the Atlantic on the way to America were diverted to Newfoundland, Halifax or other parts of Canada.

A friend of mine shared her surreal experience with me. The captain called her from the cockpit to say that the United States had been under attack by terrorists who'd taken control of planes that flew into buildings killing everyone on board. She and her crew were told to take their jump seats and arm themselves with whatever they could think of—knives, empty wine bottles, anything that could hurt someone trying to overtake them and cockpit crew. The captain made announcements to advise passengers what was happening. They were to remain seated for the remainder of the flight.

They landed in Newfoundland a few hours later.

Lisa said, "We had a full flight, over two hundred people. We must have sat on the tarmac for hours when we landed, I don't remember how long, but it was a long time until we realized we wouldn't be released to fly soon. We'd been grounded indefinitely. There were no hotel rooms. Several planes landed before we did."

Her crew and the passengers were put up in a convent with cots to sleep in. It was already getting cold in Newfoundland in September, and there was no heating.

"It was the most unforgettable experience, one that I'll remember for the rest of my life. It was a terrible thing to happen. But I believe in the love of humanity after that incident," she said. "People shared clothing to keep warm. We prayed together. Strangers merged to become one big family. The nuns bonded with all of us. We kept being encouraged that this would pass. Several nuns in a choir sang for us. We cried."

Nuns to the rescue—I loved that. It brought back memories of the nuns in my school in Rome. Kind, loving and benevolent women serving God and humankind.

I considered myself lucky that I hadn't been stuck anywhere else but home. More stories were told about planes that had to divert from their destinations and land immediately. Passengers and flight crew pooled their resources, sharing rental cars to drive home. But cars for rent were scarce from the frenzy of demand. Flying was no longer an option for anyone. Trains were full. And some people had no way to get home without flying.

"It took several days," said one passenger. "I was stranded in Frankfurt."

"My husband was really getting worried about me. My kids are used to me being gone a certain number of days…but I was gone for a week before I finally got home," said a flight attendant.

Like most of America, we watched the news, craving for answers and any kind of information. That's all we could do. It was a helpless feeling. Heartbreaking stories began to unfold. A man who worked at the Twin Towers had called in sick and was thus spared his life. His grief turned into survivor guilt. "How and why was I spared?" he asked.

There were acts of bravery. "Let's roll" was a slogan that came from a man whose wife and children lived in Washington, D.C. Their plane went down near Pittsburgh as he and other passengers made an unsuccessful attempt to subdue the hijackers. Passengers made last minute cell phone calls home to their loved ones before crashing into the ground to their death.

Children lost parents. Families lost loved ones. Names of the flight crews that perished were shown on TV. I cried, my heart aching for them and their families. That could have been me. Although they worked for different airlines, they were like my co-workers. I couldn't imagine the terror they felt and had recurring nightmares about it.

Vivid scenes of throats being slashed and terrifying screams flashed through my mind and in my dreams. I wondered how I would have reacted to that. Would I have gone into shock or fought them? What were those last moments really like? It was all I could think about for days.

Did they feel it? I hoped that it was so sudden that they didn't understand.

But stories of people pulling together kept emerging. Heroic people on the ground in New York, rescuing fellow citizens, firefighters who'd lost their lives and loved ones.

Though I knew I'd take to the skies again, things would be much different. Security was tightened. Airport workers and crew alike looked over their shoulders with vigilance. There were long lines at security checkpoints as all travellers came under tight scrutiny. The travelling public was being tested for their patience.

Sadly, there were innocent Americans and foreigners of Muslim origin that were targeted and detained. Fear had overtaken our nation. Airports became centers of high anxiety. Fewer people flew in the days following the massacres. Airlines announced cutbacks and bankruptcies.

September 11th, 2001 marked a massive change for the airline industry, the travelling public and the lives of many people. It was the day I'll never forget.

Twenty-Two

THE LEAVE

I wondered whether my airline was going to go down the path of Eastern. Both John and I were fearful that we'd soon be out of our jobs. Airlines suffered after 911, as people had become afraid to travel. USAirways and other companies announced furloughs because of scheduling cutbacks. The future looked grim.

The airline offered voluntary leaves to avoid furloughing those who needed to keep working. We were offered several options—one, two or three years off without pay but a guarantee that we'd retain seniority and benefits and a job to return to.

"Here's the chance you've been waiting for. You can take a long leave without quitting your job," John said. I hadn't envisioned this coming about as a result of the terrorist attack. But I was thrilled at the opportunity to take some time off. Several hundred of my colleagues and I took advantage of a break from flying.

I immersed myself into painting and writing. On occasion, I'd accompany John on his trips. It was fun to fly as a passenger on his flights and spend a long layover together in Las Vegas. I took a trip with him to Munich where we took tours, ate schnitzel and drank beer.

We went to Florida and took road trips. We bought a small house in St. Augustine in the northeastern part of Florida as a getaway vacation place. We loved visiting the oldest city and its beaches. It had grown since the 1970's, but still retained its old world charm. My dream of owning a piece of this beautiful part of the world had finally come true.

I decorated it simply. Bright Florida style, each room having a different pastel color scheme. I loved that house more than any place I'd ever lived, including our beautiful and much larger home in Delaware. There was something about it that felt magical. Huge slider windows brought in lots of light, and the greenery backlit by the cerulean blue skies made for a natural work of art by God. We had a nature preserve behind us, untouched by landscapers. I imagined the famous nineteenth century watercolorist Winslow Homer being inspired by such a scene. Cardinals, squirrels, and an occasional deer paid us visits. The songbirds reminded me of the mornings I woke up in a pup tent near the beach so many years before. Frogs serenaded us by night. We were surrounded by large and small palm trees. I hadn't realized that there were so many different kinds.

The beach was a twenty-minute walk, but only a ten-minute car ride and we could drive on the sand. We often brought a picnic with us along with umbrellas and chairs. We'd spend a full day enjoying the sun and riding the waves with boogie boards and then come home to shower off the sand and take a nap. We'd cook out on the patio in the evenings.

I attended another seminar in San Francisco, called *Visions*. Barbara, the trainer, was incredibly dedicated to the participants, guiding them towards their passions. It was the last part of the seminar trilogy, designed to explore our dreams and map out bucket lists, declaring our intentions and plans for the future. One of the things I put on my poster board, called the "Visions Map" was a drawing of the state of Florida with a red heart right where St. Augustine was. I hoped that someday we'd make it our permanent home.

I was so happy to learn new things and John continued to encourage me. He enjoyed my enthusiasm. I once found a quote that said, "A healthy relationship is one where two independent people make a deal that they will help make the other person the best version of themselves." I reflected upon my gratitude for having yet one more chance at a marriage that was so wonderful.

Meanwhile job security at all the airlines continued to be at risk. John already had a real estate broker's license.

"If USAirways goes out of business, we could work in real estate together," he said. I hoped it wouldn't come to that. That would be so sad. But I decided to go to real estate school to get my sales agent's license in Florida. It was boring and hard. I had difficulty getting through it. So many laws to learn and then there was math, which I hated. I failed the first exam. But I was determined to make it on the second try. Having our own real estate company would be Plan B, a new venture for both of us.

Thankfully, however, USAirways survived. But not without pay cuts and work rule changes. The pilot and flight attendants had to agree to concessionary contracts—or there'd be no airline to work for. Thankfully we all agreed to the changes to keep our jobs. John still needed to fly, even if I decided not to return.

There were still other things I wanted to do.

A class was offered as certification to become a Life Coach. This piqued my attention. It involved helping people move forward to achieve their dreams. The coach assists the clients to see what is possible, and guides them step by step towards their goals. Conversely, psychology—which I'd always been interested in, was a conversation about the past and about healing old wounds. Coaching focused on talking about the future.

Given our experience of family breakdown to breakthrough, I could specialize in working with families whose teens were returning home from specialty programs. We'd define values and refine communication skills. Assisting to establish healthy boundaries and house rules. Would I like that better than being a flight attendant? Time would tell.

I signed up for the eight-month course. It entailed a lot of reading and research, writing and practice-coaching. I did a lot of writing in our St. Augustine home which I began to call our little "retreat". Part of the course was to hone our listening skills. In the busy world, I often found myself drifting, while supposedly listening. Was my brain in multi-task mode or did I have attention deficit? I decided it was the former not the latter. The exercise in active listening was powerful.

"What I just heard you say was you don't care about Tom's room being messy. What would be more important then?" I'd ask a lot of question that would promote my clients to think things out. Instead of telling people what to do or how to be, I was guiding them to come up with their own solutions, empowering them in getting ahead.

I had ten client families at a time. We set up weekly phone calls. That kept me busy and it was very fulfilling. But it was all phone work since they lived all over the country. I had to keep written records of the conversations, and the billing part wasn't fun. I longed for more energetic personal meetings. Nevertheless I continued, and families came to me as referrals from others who'd gained much satisfaction. I felt honored when people asked me to be their family coach.

A few months later I had another opportunity to learn how to become a seminar facilitator. It was an intensive course. I joined the class and began the grueling process of—once again—tackling the demons that invaded each time I'd stand up to speak in front of my peers or in public. Perfection issues, fear, approval needs. Do those ever go away? I learned that they never do; you just have to be aware of them and put them in abeyance. Fear? Oh, did I forget that I could turn that energy into excitement?

I discovered that large group facilitation was not my forte. To work such a job meant being away from home more than I ever was. However, the learning did provide me with the tools to produce a small group workshop of my own, entitled "Graceful Aging" for women. It was successful and fun. The premise was to acknowledge the aging process, not fight it as many do, but to embrace it. To rid oneself of emotional burdens, practice forgiveness and write down one's passions, and goals still left unrealized. No matter what our age, my desire was to instill that the world is still a playground where dreams can still come true.

Throughout this time I painted. It was a soothing outlet and I felt centered while playing with watercolors. John suggested I show my art publicly. My framer offered me his shop to exhibit my paintings. We invited friends and acquaintances for an evening of wine and cheese. We had soft music playing in the background. I sold all the paintings. There were a couple I had marked "not for sale" though—they held sentimental value. One was a scene of our back porch in Ft. Lauderdale with vivid tropical greenery. The other was a painting of our northern home in Delaware in the snow. I will never sell those.

I wasted no time and accomplished all the things my heart yearned for that my flying career had denied. I was grateful for having been given this freedom. I learned so much in those three years.

I realized though, that I still missed flying. I knew I'd look forward to going back to my favorite career of all. The break that I so badly needed reinforced my desire to return to the skies. I suspect that not many people had the opportunity to explore other careers like I did.

I visited my mother in Greece a few times. I wished USAirways would fly there. Trips to visit mom could be more frequent and I could even work those since I spoke the language. Maybe someday. My mother and I often talked about it.

"Wouldn't it be fun to see each other every week?" I said.

"It would be a dream come true," was her reply.

I saved money by doing my own hair color and rarely visited a salon except for an occasional hair cut. But the gray roots kept popping up more and more frequently. One day as I was dying those pesky roots at the hairline dark brown, I noticed how badly I trashed the bathroom. It was always such a messy endeavor. There was brown hair dye all over the sink, the floor and splatters of it even made it to the mirrors. The clean-up was a hassle. Worse than chocolate syrup, this stuff had a way of staining the porcelain sink. I scrubbed it for hours with bleach. It wasn't just a matter of tedious work on the roots of my hair, which took at least an hour, but cleaning it all up afterward—that was a pain. And the gray hair popped up more frequently now. I was doing the dye job twice a month. It was time consuming dirty work.

"I am so sick of dying these roots. It's driving me crazy. They grow so fast that I have to do it almost weekly." I whined.

"I've been trying to tell you for a long time, you ought to let it grow out and quit dying it," John said.

I'd been dying it for so long—ever since I was twentyish—just to experiment with different colors. There were times I'd had jet black, blond and finally red hair. My favorite was "Red Oak" by Clairol, a rich brownish auburn. It went so well with my red lipstick and my complexion, as well as the navy blue uniform.

Flying was my reason to keep up the haircoloring, since I was always into glamour, make-up—anything that I thought would enhance my appearance as much as I could. I recalled Eastern's makeover class in which Miss Ginny said "You're on stage..."

I was fifty, but I looked younger. What would gray hair make me look like?

138

The thought scared me. What if it looked bad? Made me look old?

But I wasn't flying, so I had no excuses. I needed to give it a try. I was curious. So I started letting my roots grow out which made me look like a skunk. I had a whitish-silver band at the part line with the rest of my hair dark brown. Maybe cutting it all off, short would do it. But I quickly dismissed the thought. Too drastic. I was very much attached to my long locks.

But I'd reached the end of my patience. I was a slave to my hair in the name of vanity. I was ready to take a leap of faith. Maybe it would look like John's. His hair was an enviable blend of silver and gray. But men always looked distinguished. What about women?

When I confided in my girlfriend Tisha, she said, "Just try it. I think you'd look great. You can always change it back if you don't like it. Imagine what it would be like not having to dye your hair all the time!"

I made an appointment first thing in the morning so as not to change my mind with a stylist who specialized in sassy short hairdo's. I'd seen his work on a woman who worked at the doctor's office, liked it and asked her for his name.

I couldn't sleep the night before the appointment. How vain. It's only hair. People lose hair in illnesses. You're bigger than that, I told myself. My mind was in full throttle. I tossed and turned. When morning finally came I said, "I can't go through with this."

Although I knew better, I felt as if my long brown locks were part of my identity. It scared me to reveal the grays in the form of a very drastic short haircut—even a cute sassy short style. No. I wasn't going to do it. Damn my ego—I should know better. Hair is not one's identity.

"Oh yes you are. You were *excited* about this yesterday, Sheika. What happened?"

"I...cccan't."

"You're being unreasonable. You've been to all those trainings where you had to get out of your comfort zone and stretch. You felt good about that. Think about it," said John.

We kept on arguing, but I knew there was no going back. I'd thought about it for too long. I finally surrendered to curiosity again.

While I took my shower that morning I could feel my stomach flipping about. I washed my long locks one last time, wondering what it would feel like with practically no hair on my head.

I got in the car and sat silently, staring out in front of me, as John drove me to the salon. "You know I love you and I think you are beautiful no matter what. If you don't like it, just dye it again," he said.

At the hair studio I met the stylist, who seemed overzealous and high on amphetamines. The salon reeked of chemical smells, rotten eggs and ammonia. He was wearing a black shirt and his blue jeans had holes in them. His hands were shaking. *Oh God.*

I surrendered to the cutting. He worked fast, his hands deftly manipulating the scissors. I felt clumps of hair fall off my shoulders and onto the floor. My heart pounded heavily. Thoughts invaded my mind. What if I look like a pin-head?

When he was done, he held up a mirror behind me so that I could look at myself three-dimensionally. What I saw was a new me. I was smiling. And I loved my new haircut, shiny silver and short.

I knew that I'd never revisit the Miss Clairol red oak hair dye again. That relationship was over. I could hardly wait for it to grow out, longer silver gray strands.

That was one of my scariest of endeavors while on leave. Hair can become a key factor in one's identity. In later years I read the book, *Going Gray,* by Anne Kreamer, which further validated my decision. I learned that the outer image is not the true persona and embraced my authentic self. I'd done so much. Gone to school. Coached individuals and families. Talked in seminars. Gotten a real estate license. Had my own art exhibit. But the day I saw a new me with gray hair in the mirror. It felt magical. I felt free.

Twenty-Three

THE COMEBACK

I t was time to fly again. I was excited. I'd played at a lot of things. It was a chance many people aren't afforded. I got to see if the 'grass was really greener' on the other side of my fence. It wasn't. I missed flying and serving people while visiting other cities.

I also liked the way the blue uniform looked with my silver-gray hair.

"Mary—it looks great!" said Tisha. "I don't even think you need to grow it long!" But I missed it being long.

I soon learned how the airline business model had changed. We wouldn't be serving hot meals anymore on domestic flights. Alcohol on international flights was no longer gratis. Things changed in the entire industry—not just USAirways. Some flight attendants thought it was ludicrous. Others embraced it.

"It's not so bad—actually our job has become easier," my friend Terry said. "Remember? We used to serve a hot meal on every flight that was more than one hour and thirty minutes' duration. It was a lot of work when we did Philly-Ft. Lauderdale turns." Now if passengers wanted to eat, they had to purchase their snacks. Alcohol prices were raised to seven dollars for beer, wine or liquor. Soft drinks remained free of charge.

"It makes sense. Tickets have become less expensive. We have to make it up somewhere," said another colleague who did some union work. "There's been lots of changes. Wait until you see your first paycheck."

I was eager to get back on the planes and glad to have the airline job to come back to. My co-workers had endured two bankruptcies while I was on leave. I missed flying with John and some of my fellow crewmembers. I felt a sense of gratitude for the people who kept things going, persevering through it all.

There had been labor strife. Concessionary contracts had to be negotiated between management and the union groups consisting of pilots, flight attendants and machinists. There were massive pay cuts and loss of retirement benefits, as we knew them. Retirement annuities had been handed over to the government to manage, the PBGC, (Pension Benefit Guarantee Corporation). Medical insurance premiums were higher. Anyone who had come into the airline industry with certain career expectations suffered major disappointment. We were no longer riding the gravy train of a job with handsome benefits that paid great dividends. Thankfully we had 401k options and other means to plan for the future. It no longer would be cushioned by a generous airline retirement.

The benefits however, were still better than what most companies were offering. Business models were being reinvented everywhere, because the economy was at an all time low. 911 impacted all businesses—not just airlines.

I went to the mandated five-day training to re-qualify for my job. I'd been out for too long to just take a one-day refresher course. Those of us returning from extensive leaves had to undergo a more detailed review.

There were six of us in the class. We'd all done similar things during our leaves—checked out other possibilities in the 'real' world. Some quit while several of us came back eagerly ready to fly again. We were a happy bunch in the classroom, seated at a large round table.

"It's so nice to see a group of happy people," said one of the instructors.

"What's not to be happy about?" I asked.

"There's a lot of depression out there. Things have changed," said another instructor. "But things will get better."

I found out how my co-workers had endured the 911 fallout. The bankruptcies had forced catering to eliminate such things like bags of pretzels for the beverage service. Passengers complained. Flight attendants were now responsible for cleaning the aircraft after each leg as contract cleaners had been dismissed as cost cutting measures. I dreaded cleaning the plane. Passengers always left such a mess.

"We make announcements to ask passengers to hand over their cups and cans and other trash before landing now," Terry informed me.

It was an education I wasn't embracing easily. But I was still cautiously optimistic.

"Some of us had to beg for more ice to make it through each leg," Tisha said. "Sometimes we ran out of stuff and we just had to make do. Catering didn't replenish supplies regularly."

The employees of USAirways from top to bottom were my new heroes. We were glad that we had a corporate leadership culture that wasn't eager to sell us out. Instead, they worked at finding ways to survive and grow, become better and competitive. A merger with United Airlines was announced which we thought might save us. We hoped for the best but there were anti-trust issues. The fear mongers in Washington, DC deemed it wasn't plausible and might not be good for the travelling public. So USAirways had to go at it alone.

Cleaning the aircraft wasn't so bad. Provisioning was getting better and I felt that we had a chance at surviving, maybe thriving even. Most of us were optimistic like that. I didn't feel as I did before I left Eastern. The reassurances by management helped morale.

When I got my first paycheck I winced, disbelieving what I saw. The give-backs were huge and my paycheck had been cut by at least one third of what I'd been used to earning. But I was doing what I loved. Money wasn't everything. Less spending power meant fewer trips to the mall. I could certainly live with that. Some people had mortgages and other higher responsibilities and I felt sympathetic towards them. I hoped that maybe someday we'd become profitable and get raises.

Management stated that we needed to merge, or be acquired, or acquire another airline. The seemingly perfect fit showed up soon enough. Another airline, America West, was suffering from the same economic woes. It made sense to merge and grow larger. The federal government approved this one. American West's new CEO, Doug Parker, became the leader of our combined airline. A new sense of enthusiasm filled the air.

The airline industry slowly began to pick up. The fears of air travel were replaced by confidence. People relied on the airways to get to places quickly.

Al Qaeda couldn't take that away from the western world. Security had been tightened and airplanes began filling up.

Going through security was an ordeal for the passengers. I wanted to make them feel at home and comfortable once they'd reach my plane—they'd often had to run and were huffing and puffing down the jet way. People then learned to allow more than an hour to get from the airport entrance onto their flights. But in spite of these difficulties it was good to see the gain in consumer confidence.

I offered my experience in training facilitation and coaching and wrote short inspirational articles for the monthly flight attendant newsletter. Because I had some teaching experience through the courses I'd taken, I was invited to join the training department as the two airlines merged. Both had to become consistent with service, but most importantly with FAA procedures in order to acquire the single operating certificate to become one airline.

Procedures were changed and adopted on both sides. I was sent to Phoenix where the America West flight attendants were based to teach new ways of doing the same job. America West trainers came to the east side to teach at USAirways' training center. It was fun getting to meet new faces. But sometimes it was challenging, like teaching old dogs new tricks.

"That doesn't make sense—why change the way we evacuate?" asked a student.

"And now the lead can go to the back of the plane during flight? We weren't allowed to do that—we couldn't walk past the wings," said another.

"Well now the lead can go to the rear galley when necessary," I said.

On the West side, the lead had to remain close to first class during the entire flight. All airlines have different rules that flight attendants must follow. Old habits were hard to change, but enthusiasm prevailed.

As an example, America West called their lead the number one flight attendant. USAirways' lead was the "A". The combined airline adopted the A, B, and C method rather than calling each other one, two or three. That was the simpler of the revised procedures.

There were new aircraft being delivered—the Airbus A321 that my West colleagues needed to learn. It was one of my favorite modules to teach. Part of it was classroom work. We spent the afternoon isn't he plane's mock-up to practice drills and other scenarios.

My schedule became a mix of part-time flying and training and I enjoyed doing both. I was glad to be in the skies again, but eager to use some acquired skills from the leave that I'd taken. Making required training a pleasant interactive experience, I worked alongside some phenomenal teacher-colleagues from both America West and USAirways.

Tisha and I often worked together as trainers. We were assigned to do service training when the company revised business class service procedures on the transatlantic routes. The wide-body dual aisle aircraft had carts with preset trays that we presented to the passengers at chair side, directly from carts. We'd "dress" the salad for them and offer wine and bread starting at the first row of seats and going aft. Some of the cynics amongst us didn't appreciate having to learn a new serving procedure. They dubbed that class "salad training day." But service was being revamped as the airline emerged out of bankruptcy. The business model had changed, but there'd be new designs and ways to serve—and more training.

An offer came to do full time training. I was flattered. I enjoyed being in the classrooms and the airplane mock-ups with my colleagues. I liked using the tools I'd learned during my leave of absence. The evaluation feedback from students praised me. I was good at it. I engaged my students so that enthusiasm replaced boredom.

But would that be enough to satisfy me?

After much thought, and a lot of journaling, I decided that flying was the lifestyle I really missed while I was grounded. I was meant to fly.

Twenty-Four

THE THEME PARK TRAVELERS

I flew domestic trips before going back to flying International. I knew I wanted to work the transatlantic trips again, but thought it would be better to do the shorter ones first. Returning to the skies exhausted me. I'd forgotten what it was like to be on my feet for so many hours and move about the plane pushing and pulling carts. Certain muscles in my body showed their presence at the end of my trips in the form of aches and pains.

I'll get used to it again. Thankfully my exercise routine helped get me through the transition.

Meanwhile John and I had a day trip together flying to Orlando. Philly-Orlando-Philly. We checked in, met our crew and began to receive the passengers. As I greeted people during boarding, I noticed a passenger's bare feet propped up on the first class bulkhead wall. Didn't anyone travel with manners anymore? I missed the days when people dressed well and were polite when flying. Just as I was about to tell Mr. Barefoot very nicely to remove his feet from the carpeted bulkhead wall, the interphone rang.

"Yes, this is Mary," I said.

"Mary, this is Beth in the back. We have no more room for luggage."

"Okay, I'll get an agent to start tagging and checking bags. Thanks." People brought whatever they could onto the plane since there was a fee charge to check bags, part of the new business model that contributed to good profits. I wondered how these passengers could afford Orlando vacations.

Airfares and theme park fees had gotten expensive. When I was a tour guide the cost for park entry into Walt Disney World was eight dollars per person. Now the cost was almost a hundred per—and that didn't include food or drinks.

We had a full flight. It was a party crowd, animated and chatty, excited to be going on vacation. I noticed passengers reading travel books.

"Are you excited? I asked a family with four children. They nodded gleefully.

"It's our first time to Disney World," said the dad. "We're going to do it all, Sea World, Universal Studios—the works."

"Oh great, you're going to have lots of fun," I said. "Don't forget to wear sunscreen." They looked so white I could almost see through their skin to their blue veins. During the flight I went over to them and gave them some tips for their itinerary in the Magic Kingdom. I'd been there at least 700 times and knew the short cuts.

"Check for the parade times and plan your day around them," I told them the best spot to be during the parade, at the center circle in front of Cinderella's castle. "That way you're centrally located in between all the lands. If you head into Tomorrowland you'll have no wait times to get on the rides. The parade will still be going on as it heads into the other direction ending in Frontierland."

"Be sure to have a drink at the top of the Contemporary Hotel. It's a monorail ride to get there, but the view is beautiful," I told the parents. They thanked me. Nice looking family, I thought. Polite kids. Neatly dressed. I made sure they knew how much I appreciated the children saying "please" and "thank you." Sometimes kids weren't as well behaved.

We landed, got refueled and re-catered. We tidied up the plane, the new flight attendant responsibility. Trash was everywhere, on the floors and seats. Candy wrappers. Cheerios had to be swept up. One family left a dirty diaper in the seat-pocket. Thankfully we were provisioned with plastic gloves for these endeavors. You never know what you might find.

"Geez—how many times did we walk through collecting trash?" asked one of my crew rhetorically.

I took a minute to go outside and breathe in some Florida air. It was nice and warm. I missed the balmy weather and perpetual greenery. Palm trees around the airport swayed with a light breeze. The sky was bright blue. Maybe someday we'd move back to the Sunshine State.

Our return flight from Orlando was also booked full.

Children boarded the plane wearing Mickey Mouse ears and Pluto hats and moms and dads looked spent as they corralled their broods into their assigned seats. They were sunburned, for the most part, and returning to the thirty-five degree cold in the north wearing shorts and t-shirts.

When John made the announcement about the flight and weather in Philly there was an audible "ugh" to be heard.

"Did you get to see Mickey Mouse?" I asked one of the children. Shy, she nodded 'yes' and clung to her mom's skirt, burying her face in it.

The gate agent came up to the boarding door, ready with baggage tags in hand, a customary event. The remaining passengers standing in line were not happy.

"Hey I purposely just packed a *small* roll aboard suitcase, I know it fits in the overhead space." one of them said.

"We realize that, but unfortunately there is no more overhead space." Couldn't they part with it for just a few hours? But I empathized, knowing that it was a hassle to retrieve luggage at baggage claim. They wanted to get off the plane and out of the airport as quickly as possible and I couldn't blame them.

A woman came onto the plane wearing a low cut dress with two huge caricature-like boobs. It was like a Disney cartoon image. Except that Disney didn't make booby cartoons. A feast for the eyes of the male flight attendant standing next to me, this chick got more than her money's worth—which was not always a good thing when it came to plastic surgery by an overzealous surgeon.

"Can you throw this away?" Ms. Silicone handed me an empty Starbucks cup.

"Of course," I said. She was accompanied by her beau who was wearing flip-flops and stylishly torn jeans. Both of them seemed very friendly. We were at a standstill as the agent tagged bags as the never-never land crowd of fantasy travelers settled in. That's when I took advantage of small talk with the peeps.

"Did you have a nice vacation?" I asked them.

"Oh yes, it was our honeymoon; we did all the theme parks and stayed on Disney property. It was great." I made a mental note to offer them complimentary wine later.

Finally, with boarding complete, we were on our way. As I looked over at the sea of faces our plane was full of people of all shapes, sizes and ethnicities. That's what I loved about my job, seeing and meeting people from all over the world. I did have some pet peeves. Some parents didn't teach good manners to their children. When I'd ask a child what they'd like to drink.

"Coke." No 'please'. Just "Coke" as they were immersed into their electronic gizmos. Often times I didn't get a "thank you" either. When children *do* say please and thank you, I praise them *and* the parents.

Some people didn't pay attention to the safety demo—another pet peeve within the flight attendant ranks. Complacency is often interrupted whenever an incident occurs, like the Miracle on the Hudson when Captain Sully glided a plane to a safe landing—or after 911. But many times, passengers can be heard carrying conversations or reading newspapers when it'd be better to pay attention to safety briefings.

When we began the beverage service, a passenger's call-bell rang. I went to the corresponding seat and found a distraught woman.

"I want to change my seat," she whispered in my ear.

"Can you wait?" I asked her. "We've got carts in the aisle at the moment."

"No." She shook her head. It was clear she wanted out of that middle seat. I assumed she wanted to sit at an aisle. There were no aisle seats but she said she didn't mind, she just wanted to move. We accommodated her request swiftly. She had a frown on her face and shook her head at me. I made a mental note to talk to her—later. Right then, we needed to complete the service. The theme park vacationers were getting quite demanding. They wanted their cocktails and pretzels.

I gave the honeymoon couple some complimentary wine and congratulated them.

"Thank you so much!" they said. They were snuggled up close together, holding hands.

Some passengers were deep asleep, oblivious to drinks or noise, obviously spent of all their energy.

When we finished our service, one of the flight attendants asked me why the woman wanted to move all of a sudden.

"I don't know, maybe she wanted to be closer to the front of the plane, I'll ask her later." I said.

We tidied up the plane, getting ready for approach and landing. The lady who'd moved earlier was standing in front of the lavatory, waiting her turn. It was the perfect opportunity to chat with her.

"Was there something wrong with your seat?" I asked.

"No, there was nothing wrong with the seat. But the man sitting next to me at the window, he was weird."

"Oh?" My interest was piqued.

"Well I don't know how to say it. But he was reading a pornographic magazine and fondling himself. He had his jacket over his lap and was, you know…masturbating."

"Oh no! I had no idea. I wish you had told me—I would have said something to him," I said.

At the end of the flight I looked for him to warn him about his disruptive behavior. I wasn't sure how I was going to reprimand him, but I was going to tell him that it was inappropriate to do what he did on an airplane.

He walked off the plane, avoiding eye contact, refusing to talk to me. One by one each passenger deplaned, the goofy, the sleepy, the cheery, the wild and the uncouth.

I shared the story with my flight crew and John. We busted out laughing even though it was rather a disgusting story and we were tired. After those trips my routine was to pour myself a glass of wine and soak in a hot tub.

Theme park people and crazies. Gotta love them.

Twenty-Five

ATHENS BOUND

In 2007, my heart soared with a long awaited announcement: USAirways would begin flying to Athens, starting in May, and there was a need for Greek speakers.

I called my mother immediately.

"Mom—it's what we've been waiting for!" I said excitedly. We both cried happy tears.

"Oh how wonderful!" she said.

I danced a happy jig across my living room. The time had come for me to fly across the Atlantic again. I was anxious to see my mother on a regular basis. I'd become jealous of people who lived close to their parents. An annual vacation to travel to Greece simply wasn't enough. She was getting older and so was I. Papa had passed on years earlier from lung cancer. The older I got, the more I appreciated how the years flew by and how much I'd missed her. It reminded me of how much she'd missed her own mother after marrying Papa and moving to Brazil in 1945. It took fourteen years for them to reunite. At least I'd had the annual visits…

"Pernane ta chronia," she'd tell me over the phone, *"The years are passing."*

In my younger years I'd dismiss her words, being afflicted with what young people suffer from—the illusion that there's always plenty of time. There isn't. My mother was showing signs of aging. I knew she wouldn't be around forever.

Reflecting upon my upbringing, I realized how fortunate I'd been to experience cultural differences and travel the world. To learn foreign languages and see so many places. I'd taken this for granted.

Now I could hardly wait to have the small Greek flag pinned on my uniform and be the foreign destination speaker on flights to Athens. No way would I be able to fly those trips otherwise. The average seniority that went to international flying was forty years. By then I'd been flying half that amount of time. Foreign speakers, however, were welcomed at any seniority level. We were a minority.

I had to take a language test. I'd passed the French and Italian ones but I knew this one wasn't going to be as easy even though I could speak everyday Greek. There was a different alphabet to contend with, and lots of technical terms. I wouldn't be ready for awhile. But at least I could practice. The hardest part was learning to read Greek. Up until then I was able to read capital letters on signs, but not text. It would be a challenge but I was up for it.

I asked my supervisor for two sets of announcement booklets and sent one to my mother. On twice-weekly phone calls I'd read them to her and she'd correct my pronunciation at various points. Finally I felt that I'd become proficient enough. I was confident to take the trip to Berlitz in New York to get tested.

On a cold and rainy day I took the Greyhound bus from Wilmington to Manhattan. I knew New York City well after so many layovers there. I got my bearings when I ventured outside the Central Station and easily found my way to Berlitz's offices.

When I arrived I was asked to take a seat in the waiting room. I felt nervous. Finally I was called over to meet my examiner.

"*Kalimera sas,*" I said to him in Greek. "Good day." We shook hands. He was serious and appeared to mean business.

It was a grueling test lasting ninety minutes. One hour of conversation in the beginning, the last thirty minutes entailed a series of specific questions that were pertinent to flying—typical ones a passenger might ask. Such as, "what type of juices do you have?" or "what if I don't make my connection because of this delay?" My responses seemed to satisfy Mr. Tester.

The top score was a five. Minimum passing score was four. I'd passed both the French and Italian tests easily with a 4.5. Berlitz was very strict.

"In time, as you fly more, your vocabulary will get better," he said, as he scribbled notes in his yellow legal writing pad. When it was over we shook hands and told me it would take a couple of weeks to get my score. That seemed like an eternity, but I found out sooner than two weeks.

I'd barely passed this test but was grateful to squeeze by. The airline needed Greek speakers and gave me a reprieve. I hadn't spoken the language for so long and knew that I'd get much better. I insisted that every phone conversation with my mother should be in Greek. It took getting used to because we'd spoken English at home all the time.

The other Greek speakers and I became close and shared similar experiences with the testing. They'd started before me, and acted as my mentors.

Athens was a long hard flight. Ten hours from Philly and almost eleven hours on the return. Filled with cruise people and vacationers, some of whom were like the Theme Park People, except that I had a long relationship with them because of the extended time together in flight. That was good—and bad. The good was, I loved getting to know them, form a sort of camaraderie with some. I wanted to know where they were from. Were they going on vacation? Many went to visit family in the homeland. But when you had a miserable complainer you were stuck with them for the duration. Holiday travel entailed large families with understandably restless children who liked running around and getting in our way. It couldn't be helped, but it wasn't ideal. As flight attendants we have to grin and bear such things.

I felt wretched towards the end of the flights. My makeup felt like it was some kind of oily glue pasted on my face. My teeth desperately needed a good brushing even though I'd taken the time to brush them during the flight. My eyes felt scratchy. I longed for a bed to take a short nap that would refresh me for the remainder of the layover.

Landing in Greece for the first time as a working flight attendant made me feel proud. I'd come full circle and now I'd fly there several times monthly, visit my mother, enjoy the country's lively people and dine on delicious food. It was my time to reclaim the place I loved, but left behind so hastily to become independent, although I had no regrets. I was grateful to have this gift to be there on a regular basis during spring and summer months.

When I visited my mother, we talked about love, marriage, divorces and strife. Of course, she'd forgiven me my escape of 1971. I already knew that, but it felt good to really feel it and hear it in her words, to see her joy when we were together.

"I was sad when you left me. But I know you're happy and I'm happy for you. A mother wants her children to be happy and independent," she said. I shared how sorry I had been when Pamela had rebelled claiming her own independence. A mother's love is unique like no other.

In addition to seeing my mother, I found some old high school friends who were still residing in Athens. The World Wide Web and emailing had arrived, but not everyone had computers. I still had phone numbers and we corresponded by old-fashioned airmail. We arranged to meet at tavernas around the city to catch up with our life stories. Like me, there'd been marriages, divorces and children. Disappointments and pleasures, failures and accomplishments.

I wished our Philly-Athens flights weren't seasonal. When the spring and summer months ended, I went back to flying domestically again. It was a nice change, but I preferred international flying. Instead of flying multiple segments, it was one flight out and then back, with a long layover in Europe. I hoped to finish out my career doing this rather than hopping around the U.S.A.

A couple of months later I was able to fill a vacant position as a French speaker for the Paris and Brussels flights. Those became my destinations during the fall and winter months until May rolled around when Athens flying would resume.

Twenty-Six

TRANSITIONS

*A*s I began my routine flying to Paris and Brussels, I received a phone call. The training department needed people who lived in base to teach flight attendants how to use new manual credit card scanners. The airline was going "cashless" for inflight sales of liquor, beer and wine. The planes would be equipped with these new machines that everyone needed to learn how to use. I thought they were quite nifty.

The job entailed part-time teaching duty in the crew rooms where crewmembers could operate the machines hands-on. This seemed intriguing, so I accepted the assignment.

Although some flight attendants were eager to learn to use these machines, not everyone was excited about them. I heard the buzz on a daily basis.

"What else are they going to have us do? I didn't sign up for this when I started flying."

"I'm electronically-challenged. I hate computers."

"This is stupid. It's going to slow things down while delivering beverages to the passengers."

It amazed me how many crewmembers had difficulty adapting to change, in an industry that was in a constant state of flux. Most embraced it, however, thrilled at not having to collect cash that we had to deposit after each trip.

"Just think, you can go straight home after your flight—no more walks to the other end of the airport to deposit money," I said.

155

"Remember, we resisted electronic bidding. I'm glad we don't bid on paper anymore," said another flight attendant. Indeed, we'd come a long way from the archaic methods. The electronic age was in full swing.

"We have cell phones now. That's a big life changing improvement," said one flight attendant. "Remember carrying beepers?"

I did this job for a few weeks and didn't fly much. It was a change of pace that I welcomed, going home every night and sleeping in my own bed. Making a routine out of cooking dinners was interesting—I'd been used to eating out on layovers so we had to get creative. John continued flying but he chose to fly day trips so we'd both be home together in the evenings. So this is what the nine-to-five crowd did, I thought. It was fine for a short while although flying was what I was clearly born to do.

It was during that time that my mother became ill. She'd had surgery on her back that hadn't been properly performed. She had to have a second procedure. That one worked. We were happy for her success. But it didn't last. She felt well for the first couple of weeks and then developed flu-like fevers and tremors. She contracted MRSA, a potentially deadly infection that was running rampant in hospitals all over the world. We were devastated and sad. How could one get sick in a hospital? Could she fight this in her old age?

Unfortunately the Athens summer flying was over and I was frustrated at not having non-stop flights to be at her side. I was able to fly to Frankfurt and connect with another airline, and went back and forth a few times. My brother and sister flew over on several occasions as well. Mother was unconscious in an induced coma, in an intensive care unit hooked up to IV's that delivered the strongest of antibiotics. I cried when I first saw her lying there, helpless. I took her hand and whispered in her ear.

"Mom, I love you so much. I want you to know you're the best mother I could ever have had. You mean so much to me. Be strong and get well."

Was there a flutter of eye movement behind the eyelids? Tears streamed out of them. I was sure that she heard me. Could she make it? The prognosis was grim.

We lost our mother that December of 2009. Her frail body was unable to fight the devastating disease. I got the cell phone call from my brother Chris as I was teaching in the crew room that day. I broke down and cried. I'd never see my mother again. She was seventy-nine and had always led an active life. She walked everywhere as most Europeans do. I admired her for being a "young" seventy-something, always full of energy.

I reflected upon the woman that she was. My mother embraced the life of travelling the world with her brood, creating our spaces called home so lovingly no matter where we lived. She was a homemaker extraordinaire who never stopped nurturing us.

USAirways gave John and me confirmed passage to Athens. I will never forget the compassion of the flight office staff as they made the arrangements for us to leave quickly.

"Your seats are confirmed. Take as much time as you need. God bless," said my supervisor.

We flew from Philadelphia to Munich and connected on another airline bound for Athens. I was distraught and couldn't sleep during the trip, my brain going full speed. Feeling wretched upon arrival, we hailed a cab to take us to the old neighborhood, the last one I'd lived in before leaving home for good and the one I revisited frequently during my Athens flying.

I'd never been to a Greek Orthodox funeral. It was very lengthy. The priests chanted in ancient Greek and wore elaborate garments trimmed in gold threading. The church was beautifully decorated with icons of the Holy Family, Mother Mary and various saints. My mother's coffin stood in the middle of the church nave and we stood around it. It was closed, thankfully. I couldn't bear the thought of seeing her as a lifeless body. There was incense and candles cast a soft flow throughout. It felt surreal. This couldn't be happening. My heart ached knowing that I'd never see her again. At least not in this world. My feet hurt and I felt guilty for even thinking about that.

We walked in procession to the gravesite. She was buried in a crypt with her mother and father in the first cemetery of Athens.

"She'll always be with you," someone said. It gave me little comfort.

I didn't know what it would feel be like, flying back to Athens after my mother's death. During the summer prior, John and I had taken my mother to one of her favorite taverns in Glyfada. We always did something different, but mostly visited at her house. I am grateful to have had those times together. But now she was gone. Would I ever see her again? I desperately wanted to believe in the afterlife.

When May came along I dreaded my first trip back to Athens. During the boarding process I my throat choked up while making the Greek announcements and my eyes flooded with tears that I was trying to hold back. I could hear my mother's voice in my mind. Correcting my pronunciation as she did during those tutorial phone calls.

Landing was bittersweet. I basked in the comfort of having John with me as the captain. I had friends and other family members I could visit, but it wouldn't be the same with my mother gone. Each time I'd pass the old neighborhood with John, I recalled the rebellious teen that I'd been. I told him more stories about my doting parents. About our conversations. My mother's loving advice. Her disappointments with some of my choices, but also her never-ending encouragement. I'd come a long way since those days and had no regrets, except that I wish I'd visited my parents more frequently. I wish I'd told my parents more often that I loved them.

I had John. My daughter and grandchildren. Abundance. Now I was the senior matriarch, the oldest sibling, a mother and grandmother of four beautiful little girls. I'd become Yaya Mary like my own Yaya Mary who'd also passed years earlier.

How many years did I have left? And what is the meaning of death? Why must things change?

Transition is the ebb and flow of life.

Twenty-Seven

DARK CONVERSATIONS

I turned my head on the pillow to find a cooler spot for the other side of my face. Maybe then I could go back to sleep. Traversing time zones messed with me.

Was I over tired? Not tired enough? No. For sure it wasn't that I wasn't tired enough. I'd crossed to a seven-hour time difference in Athens already a few times that month. I lay in the dark wondering what to do next.

I tossed around throwing the sheets off of me, then back on again. Feeling hot. Then cold.

I didn't dare look at the digital LCD clock on the nightstand. I'd turned it to face the wall as soon as I'd checked in to the hotel room. Knowing what time it was would cast a worse spell on this condition of sleeplessness. It would make me wonder what time it was at home, and the calculating would begin to boot up other parts of my brain. Then I'd think some more about home, which would definitely make me wide awake. No. I needed to settle down back to slumber-land.

That evening, John and I snuggled together to get seven hours of sleep before flying back to the U.S. I had felt content. The hotel room was chilled the way we liked it for good sleeping. We'd had a nice day and a beautiful evening. The falling asleep part was easy. We tired ourselves out strolling around the city. But although I fell sound asleep right away, I was awake within two hours. I lay there thinking about the trip across the Atlantic, a ten-hour haul.

"You two are so lucky, getting paid to travel and have fun together," friends told us. I joked about being chauffeured'to Athens for dinner on an expensive airplane. Yes we were lucky, but there was a price to pay to work these irregular hours. It was eleven p.m. in Athens, which meant that it was four in the afternoon where we lived, stateside. And my bed became the cocoon in which the best thinking parts of my brain began to churn.

Ugh! Who goes to bed at four?

Quit calculating the time zones—you'll never go back to sleep.

And so the competing voices began to have a conference. Thoughts flooded my mind.

What was on the agenda for the next few days? Should I change my dentist appointment? I hated appointments. Why did I make it for early morning instead of later in the day?

I needed to return some phone calls. There was a dinner party to go to. I'd bring the appetizer. What should it be? Smoked salmon on pumpernickel. Or maybe a fish dip. Deviled eggs? What would I wear?

Oh God—shut up brain. Stop it already.

I felt hot and once again threw my covers off completely and laid flat on my stomach on top of the sheet, naked. The cold air-conditioning caressed my back and my legs like tiny feathers. Relief. Maybe sleep would set in. But the inner conversations wouldn't go away.

Would the dinner party be dress up or casual? I must ask the hostess.

Just concentrate on the air caressing you...

It's too cold now.

No it's not.

Just shut up. Feel the coolness.

Don't you want your covers back on now?

I pulled the covers back on and succumbed to turning the clock around to look at it.

It's after one a.m. – six p.m. at home.

I rolled over and covered myself up tightly like a cocoon, defying insomnia, burying myself into the bed as if an arctic mass had entered the dark room and the covers would keep me from freezing to death. How was it that I was feeling too hot just a few minutes ago?

This scenario was thankfully sporadic. Months would go by without any sleep issues. I needed my rest. If only I had a switch I could turn on that would make me sleep—and shut those dumb voices out of my head.

I hated pills and shied away from sleep aids even though they looked enticing on TV ads. One pilot got into some trouble after taking a pill, sleep-walking naked in a hotel. Sigh. No pills for me. They made me feel groggy anyway.

Tomorrow will be better. It's always better when daylight comes, right?

You think? NO. It's going to be a full flight. Scheduled for eleven hours because of head winds this time of year. You're screwed. Really screwed...

The voices resumed their banter. The gremlins, the goblins, fairies and witches—all of them competing with endless chatter.

Pause. Ah. Reprieve. Deep breath. Peace.

But not so soon...

Did you take your vitamins today?

Oh, you forgot to make that hair appointment before you left.

Did you leave the towels in the washer again, dummy? They're going to stink if you didn't put them in the dryer.

Don't forget to send Elaine a get-well card. Poor girl. Sick with cancer. Stupid cancer. How could we not have a cure for cancer? I said a silent prayer for her. And then I asked God to please let me sleep. But He had other plans.

What else is coming up?

Massage—ah, I could use that right now. The appointment is—for what time? I took my very smart phone off the nightstand to look.

Oh good. Not until 11:00am. I'll be able to sleep in. Maybe.

You'd better put blueberries on the grocery list—you like them in your oatmeal and you always forget.

SHUT UP!

The unwelcome visitors finally went away.

I listened to the A/C's hum. The white noise was calming. But not for long.

Get up and fire up the laptop. Write. Look at Facebook. Play scrabble.

No. Sleep. You need sleep. Sleep already!!

You're gonna be like the walking dead tomorrow, ha ha.

I'll be on my feet all day.

Oh what's wrong with me?

Finally I thought I was drifting but my eyes opened again. Through the cracks of the curtain I could see the violet gray dawn approaching. It was five in the morning. I had two hours left before the wake-up call.

You're going to be tired. Deal with it—you always make it.

Just get used to being tired. That's your norm. No one will know. You're always cheerful and looking fresh.

Ugh.

Tired. Tired. Tired. You're just tired, gonna always be tired. Ha-ha.

Was the devil residing in me?

Sleep, please come. Now.

John was snoring lightly beside me. I didn't want to disturb him. The firm mattress helped diffuse the movements of my body thrashing about on my side of the bed. I was envious. But sometimes the roles were reversed and it was he who lay beside me awake, restless as I slept, oblivious.

I turned on my phone and texted my daughter to wish her a good night. It was 10:00 p.m. in Orlando.

"Goodnight, Babygirl <3"

"G'night Mom. Aren't you supposed to be asleep? Have a nice flight. Love you."

After negotiating with one inner voice after another, they magically disappeared and I finally fell into a deep dreamy slumber.

When the alarm went off, I squirmed. I felt like I'd been hit over the head with a baseball bat.

Aaaaaargh!

John got up to make coffee. I told him about my sleepless nights and the demons that kept me awake.

"It's the damn time zone thing. How're you going to manage today?" he asked.

"I'll be okay, I just need lots of coffee now—intravenously," I said, laughing.

You'll be fine, I told myself. *This happens. It's home day—you get to rest the day after you get back. Catch up on sleep.*

When we boarded the airport van, the crew shared layover stories.

"I couldn't sleep worth a damn," said Carol.

"Me neither."

162

We commiserated, then shrugged it off, saying we'd look forward to crew rest time. Crew rest entailed sitting in an upright passenger seat reserved for flight crew. An uncomfortable position to try and sleep—unless you were super tired. I knew I'd be super-tired after the first beverage and meal service, and duty free sales.

"I slept like a baby," someone else said.

"Bitch!" said Carol. We all laughed.

I visualized my home, and my cat Mango who would greet me and cuddle at our feet. In eighteen more hours I'd have a hot shower and get into my own bed with no alarm clock to set.

What went wrong? Why didn't my body shut down like it was supposed to?

I'd dealt with this in younger years, so it was nothing new. Part of a flight attendant and pilot's job is to manage exhaustion.

Managing exhaustion is one of our highest achievements.

Twenty-five years earlier, my baby Pamela had colic and kept me awake intermittently for hours. I worked many nights, travelling with people on a bus as a tour guide. Sleep deficit wasn't anything new. Just harder to deal with as I got older.

"No matter what career you choose," a friend once told me, "You'll eventually find yourself wondering what the cause of your sleeplessness is. We want to analyze what we do—our jobs, and family. But if what we do is what we love, it's good. Insomnia is part of the human condition…"

"But with sleep deprivation, I forget things and have a foggy mind," I said.

"Not to worry. You'll remember that you're doing what you love and that's what matters," she said. Would sleep deprivation kill me? And why was I worried about death?

Norman Cousins, the author of *Anatomy of an Illness* once said, "The tragedy of life is not death but what we let die inside of us while we live."

Flying and serving my passengers made me feel alive, thus making my sleepless nights worthwhile. It was that calling from a long time ago—to transport souls, serving them and visiting lots of great places.

Not being able to sleep wasn't worth losing sleep over.

Twenty-Eight

THREE TRIPS TO BRUSSELS

Trip One – 9 Days to Go

*W*hat was I thinking when I bunched three trips in a row into my schedule? I told myself that it was a small price to pay for having extra time off to play in Florida.

Five weeks off was totally worth it. It's what flight attendants get to do, a perk of the job. Trip trade, re-adjust work schedules to maximize time off. No monthly schedule was ever the same for me. It was a heavenly arrangement; although there were times I felt restless and ready to fly.

I stayed busy as I anticipated retirement someday. But the thought of giving up my career, an eventual necessity, made me feel panicked. I was in my sixties. I probably wouldn't fly past age sixty-five even though many did. I was thankful to be blessed with great health and lots of energy.

As I prepared for my three trips to Brussels, back-to-back, my sister Pam said, "Are you crazy?"

Yes. Maybe flight attendants are…crazy.

"But I'd rather do this than sit at a desk five days a week all month. It's worth it," I said.

Mango knew I was leaving. When he saw my suitcase come out he pouted, then sat upright and stared at me, as if to say, "Do you *have to do this?*" He'd gotten used to having me around and liked it. He'd miss the morning back-scratch and the extra attention that he wouldn't get when I wasn't around.

"Oh Mango, I'll be back—you know I'll come home to you," I said in my mom-to-kitty high pitch voice that only he understood.

Separation anxiety set in. No matter what I looked forward to when it was time to fly, there was always something or someone I was leaving behind. My life at home was rich. There were friendships and social events. And my good old bed.

Get over it, it'll be okay. That was my mantra. A contrast from the days I couldn't wait to leave, when I was much younger—half my age.

John was flying with me, his schedule a bit different than mine later in the month. He would be retiring soon, so we flew together as much as we could. What would it be like flying without him? I'd gotten used to being together all the time. That was going to change in a few months.

I wondered what October days would be like in Brussels, and began to think about messed up sleep patterns coming up again. Reality sunk in. I loved my job, but I knew this was going to be a stretch. Three trips in a row would be a first. I'd never done this before. I decided I'd not stack trips together like that again. At least not three in a row...

The flights were booked full going and coming. Time for a pep talk.

After my first flight, it'll be easy again.

The flight from Philly to Brussels was uneventful, but grueling. At the end of it, my body felt like it'd been pulled through a keyhole. I felt wretchedly tired. My teeth felt like grit and slime, since I hadn't brushed them. I'd forgotten my travel toothbrush and the electric one was in my packed suitcase. I couldn't wait to get into bed when we got to the hotel where I'd get a four-hour power nap that would sustain me that afternoon and evening.

My routine was to wake up to the instant coffee that John made for me. Then I'd go to the gym on the hotel's thirtieth floor with the fabulous view. It invigorated me, bringing me back to life following that first shot of coffee. It was the European flying routine: nap on demand, force myself up, get coffee'd up, work out and go out and walk around.

I anticipated a lovely meal at Le Grand Bi, escargots and bouillabaisse, and wine. The waiter, Doriano, an Italian from Sicily, always took good care of us, starting with a complimentary glass of champagne. I was back in the groove.

165

I'd been off for awhile and it was hard getting back into the flying groove, but things were going well thus far. I don't normally drink wine and have dinner fare at 1:00pm in the U.S. But it was dark and it was dinnertime in Brussels, Belgium.

Sometimes we just can't trick our bodies—they're smarter than our brains. Just go with the flow, enjoy the moment and the evening ambiance—even it if is barely past noon in the states.

We went to bed and I was tired enough to sleep uninterrupted by insomnia, crazy voices or time warp. Instead, I had some great rem sleep and woke up feeling refreshed.

The next morning, we boarded our flight to Philadelphia, where we'd stay over to fly again the next day, trip number two. Bring it on. It was a full moon. I noticed my moods fluctuating between wanting to be home and happy to be flying.

As we prepared the plane to receive passengers, we told jokes amongst each other and drank coffee. Getting buzzed on vast amounts of caffeine was a common coping mechanism. I put my iPhone up to the public address. It played "Jet Airliner" by Steve Miller Band. My co-workers, Gina, Sue and I started dancing in the aisles like kids. I felt energized and alive again for the eight-hour flight ahead. Easy peasy. Not like ten hours from Athens. Long, but not so much.

When it was time to turn into professional adults again, flight attendants extraordinaires, I checked my lipstick and hair and took my position at the boarding door. I was ready.

Right after takeoff, an elderly man rang his call bell and asked for a cup of coffee. I poured it for him, even though we hadn't begun our beverage service and the coffee maker had barely finished brewing. He seemed desperate, and I didn't want to tell him he'd have to wait for the beverage cart to come by. I knew the 'I-need-a-cup-of-coffee-now' feeling very well.

He grabbed the cup and quickly took a sip, made an ugly sour grimace, and handed it back to me.

"American coffee is terrible," he said.

"It's probably not as good as Belgian or French coffee," I agreed.

"I hate America."

I was startled, but I ignored him.

What a sourpuss.

"I hate America," he said again.

"Then why are you going to America?" I asked.

"My children."

He became even more ornery and more vocal, until finally I had to tell him he was annoying people around him.

"Yeah. You shoulda stayed in Brussels," a man who was sitting behind him said.

Oh please. No fights.

Gina rolled her eyes. I gave her a knowing look as if to say, 'Is this guy for real?'

Shortly after the lunch service, a woman came to the rear galley.

"I have an unusual request. I need to change seats," she said.

Now? After three hours? Why? I wondered.

"I'm sorry, we only have middle seats left," I told her, shades of the Las Vegas trip masturbator crossing my mind.

"Oh that's okay. I was in a middle seat anyway. I have to move because the man next to me is wearing Depends. I think he did…number two. He stinks. Badly."

Phew. I helped her find another seat.

Poor man. He must have had surgery or a problem with incontinence. I looked over at him as he was asleep with his head against the window.

Thirty minutes later, he came to the back. I gagged at the stench but did my best not to show it.

"May I help you, sir?"

"Why did that lady next to me leave?"

I wasn't about to tell him because of his stench.

"She just wanted to move further forward, closer to the door—she has a tight connection to make in Philly," was all I could muster as I lied.

Nice job, I told myself.

"Well I want her to come back and sit next to me, we were having a nice conversation. I want her to come back."

You must have dreamed it. You were sleeping when she left…

"Well she's comfortably asleep now, sir, I don't want to disturb her."

"Oh. Well I want another seat, too. Closer to her. Or maybe you can move me up to Business Class."

Not a chance, even if I could…

"I can't do that. You have a window seat, and now no one is sitting next to you, which means you have extra room. I think you have a good situation now, sir."

He left and went back to his seat.

A few minutes later one of the other flight attendants reprimanded him for sitting in a crew jump seat that faced a row of passengers, trying to engage in conversation.

"But it's comfortable," he argued. He reluctantly went back to his seat.

That was the first trip. I was imagining the full moon wearing a great big glowing smile.

Trip Two – No Rest

The next day, I met the new crew on trip two. Some were on their second or even third go-around, like me. Some were flying up to five trips in a row. I couldn't fathom that. This was my second one; there'd be one more to go. I didn't like piling up these trips, but it was a means to an end. Time off. Many of my co-workers did this because they commuted from far away places, like California. We shared our flying stories in the briefing room as if at a cocktail party.

"Okay—no drama!" one of them said. "Let's just hope for an uneventful trip."

We laughed and headed to our plane as a jovial group of frequent flying flight crew. Once full of passengers, the plane roared up into the skies to head east again. The planes never stopped. They just went back and forth from one continent to another. They were built to do just that. This always amazed me.

"Planes don't get tired, people do," John once told me when I asked him how they kept on going. "They go through the check ups, A, B and the big one, C—the thorough check. That one is for major overhauling.

"They're just machines—not human," he said. I liked to think that they needed to go to some hangar and get some rest, an irrational thought, knowing these were flying machines. I was in awe that these mechanical birds could fly trans Atlantic incessantly.

I settled down in my jump seat to read my book. During the flight, at about ten p.m., a woman walked to the rear galley. We had finished the meal service two hours prior. She looked pale, and moved slowly. I guessed her to be about forty years old.

No wonder my attention span was lacking. I could only read one paragraph of a book—maybe a sentence or two, then I'd be interrupted…when I go back to read, I'd have to re-read where I left off.

I got up from my jump seat. My feet ached from walking through airports and the plane that day and night.

"Can I get you something?" I asked.

"I…" She fell to the floor.

I took a deep breath to control my panic as I threw my book down. Beth, who was closer to the woman kneeled next to her to check vital signs.

Was she breathing?

We responded systematically. Check for breathing, heartbeat, and call for help. We were trained in CPR should we need to use it. She had a pulse, and she was breathing. That was good news.

"Ladies and gentlemen, if there is a doctor on board, or anyone with medical experience, please come to the rear of the aircraft." I repeated the same announcement in French.

Three people came to the rear galley. One man was a veterinarian, and a woman who was a nurse. Another was a doctor. We handed them the medical kit containing a stethoscope and a blood pressure cuff in a pouch. The inside of the kit contained glucose, heart meds, an intravenous drip bag, and myriad of medications we knew nothing about, that only qualified doctors could administer. Only doctors could open and use this kit.

I called the lead flight attendant and the captain to inform them of the situation.

"Okay. Keep us informed, we'll call Med Link," the pilot said.

Med Link, a medical center that acts as a resource for airliners was located in Phoenix, Arizona. They advise the best course to follow in case of a medical emergency, and might even suggest diverting to a city close by. I hoped we didn't have to divert.

"Ah geez, I don't want to divert!" said another flight attendant echoing my sentiment.

"Me neither." But if we had to save someone's life…

We waited and watched the medical professionals. They shared information with one another. I couldn't hear what they were saying as they were kneeling down close to the woman on the floor.

"Give her some orange juice," one of them asked.

I hurried and handed it over to him.

Adrenaline was coursing through my tired body. *No drama—ha.*

The flight attendants who'd been on their rest break woke up as a result of the commotion, and announcement.

"What's going on?" one of them asked.

"She passed out. Med Link is involved. We might have to divert somewhere." I said.

"Ah crap—divert—really?"

It meant adding more hours to an already long night, and not getting to our layover until much later than usual.

Was it still a full moon out there? Yes. Ms. Moon shone brightly through the aircraft windows.

The woman slowly regained consciousness. She took a drink of the juice I'd poured. The doctor administered the drip with saline solution.

Engines kept on droning towards Brussels. We had three more hours to go.

"Her vitals are good. It appears she was dehydrated," he said.

We'd just done a water service, but she'd been asleep like most people at that hour. The cabin was dark with most of the shades down. The 'hydration service" was difficult because I was always afraid of tripping on people's legs and feet that were dangling in the aisles while I carried a tray water in plastic cups. I'd tripped before and spilled water all over a sleeping passenger once. Since then I carried a flashlight.

Passengers and flight attendants needed hydration at regular intervals in the dry environment of an airplane too. I tried to drink at least three liters a day when flying.

We were relieved that it wasn't anything more serious than a hydration issue with this woman, and relayed the information to the cockpit.

"Looks like we won't have to divert," he said.

"Who is doing the paper work?" asked the lead.

The protocol was for the first responder to gather information that we'd transfer online to a safety event reporting system. This had to be done within twenty-four hours

"Beth, I can do the online report if you'd like," I said.

"That would be great."

I wrote down the woman's name and her seat number, address and doctor's names. I included the names of all other persons involved, her condition and diagnosis according to the medical professionals.

As the doctor took her off the I.V. the woman was able to return to her seat as if nothing had happened.

I gave her a glass of water and she rested comfortably. I told her to call if she needed more to drink. We checked on her periodically, about every fifteen minutes.

The engines droned on to Brussels, slowing down for approach as we landed. The passengers walked off and the woman thanked us again as she left.

We boarded the crew van. We were quiet, staring out the windows anticipating our layover. And bed. And no more drama.

Our return trip to Philly, thankfully, was uneventful. I looked forward to a light dinner a good night's rest.

Trip Three – Belgian Chocolate

I woke up the next day feeling refreshed and ready for anything. I'd slept twelve hours. *Twelve hours!* A good night's sleep was perfect to face the last trip of the trilogy. Feeling optimistic, fatigue had been replaced with newfound energy. I looked forward to going home at the end of this nine-day marathon.

I ate a granola bar—the last one of an assortment that I carried with me in my small food bag. Eating in hotels and airplanes meant filling up on preservatives and who knew what else which caused bloating. Sometimes I couldn't avoid buying lunch at the airports or hotels, or eating the airplane food, but whenever I could I ate the stuff I brought with me.

I got creative and brought hard-boiled eggs, canned tuna, salad makings and lots of fruit. But the perishables didn't last for nine days, so at the end of my stint, it was granola bars and maybe some leftover almonds.

I brewed a small pot of coffee that was the hotel room amenity. It tasted like colored water. I missed my coffee at home, sitting near my east-facing living room window with the Florida sun streaming in. I drank two cups and then went to the hotel gym for an hour's work-out.

Philadelphia was overcast and cool that autumn day. But it was perfect weather for getting some exercise in the small hotel gym and lounging around relaxing before checking in for my trip.

I had made notes to myself on a scrap piece of paper. One was a 'home list' of things I needed to do when I got back. The other was a list of things I wanted to purchase in Brussels. Each city had its specialty. Athens had olive oil. Paris had wine. Brussels had chocolate.

I wrote chocolate on my list. Some bars of dark chocolate for me, and milk chocolate for John. And a variety box of mixed kinds with fillings of nuts and creams was always good to keep around.

I took a shower and felt refreshed as I put on my make-up. It was a good hair day. *Yessss!* I loved it when that happened. On those not-so-good hair days, I'd fuss way too long with the "damn bangs" threatening to grow them out. Worse, I'd take to them with my own scissors with bad results. But not today.

Dressed in a fresh uniform, I headed to the airport for trip number three where I ate lunch—Chinese teriyaki chicken and veggies. I wondered how much sodium it packed to bloat my tummy. We called that "jet-belly". The aircraft pressurization was the other problem, which, combined with sodium-rich food, led to water retention.

I toyed with the chicken on my plate. Someone once told me that the chicken was hit or miss. You never knew what you were really getting. I took my chances because it tasted good.

I checked in at the crew lounge computer, and met my co-workers, not knowing anyone yet. Who would I be working closely with? We signed the position chart. Mine was always the same, as the translator. Lisa was my partner on the beverage cart. The briefing went smoothly as the lead followed the checklist of items that had to be covered. Emergency manual updates, medical and evacuation procedures. Flight loads. Service. When reviewing service procedure, the aft purser Jim, who was in charge of coach, began a conversation about a different service flow than was published.

Had something changed?

Jim was a diminutive guy who looked to be around fiftyish. His carrot red hair was obviously dyed and his skin looked abused by the sun. We questioned him about his procedure. He stubbornly reiterated that his way worked, so we agreed to try it. It was no use arguing—he'd made it clear we were doing things his way.

Whatever. I just didn't want drama.

One of the flight attendants rolled her eyes at Jim. I began to feel some trepidation about this trip—before it even started.

When we began setting up the food and beverage carts, the galley turned into chaos. Lisa and I worked on stocking our beverage cart, adding extra ice and other items that we thought we might need. Typically, Brussels people like soda water, which we often ran out of. As I piled extra ones onto the cart, Jim was taking them off the cart and putting them back into compartments.

"You won't need those right now—wait until the second service," he said.

Should I argue, or ignore him?

Lisa began to speak.

"Yes we *do* need them now. Why are you worried about our beverage cart? You're on meals. Mind your own business. Set up your own cart. Get out of my way."

Uh oh.

"You'll run out and then you won't have any for later," Jim said.

"So when we run out, we run out. But they want what they want, and we should give it to them if they want it now. And why do you care? When we run out, we tell the people we don't have anymore soda water, that's all." I gathered that Lisa liked to rant. She obstinately began pulling the soda cans back out of the compartments. I added my own thoughts.

"Look Jim, everything will work out just fine, why don't you let us take what we think we'll need? It'll make the beverage service go much more smoothly."

Jim didn't respond and instead banged things around in the galley. I could almost see steam coming out of his head like in a cartoon of someone with a passive-aggressive attitude.

What a control freak.

Lisa and I finished our set-up and moved to the front of the coach section to begin serving. The intercom chimed and since I was closest to a nearby phone, I picked it up.

"Mary here."

"Mary—what are you two doing? Didn't I tell you Bev and I would go out first and the beverage cart would be in *front* of the meal cart?" Jim shouted impatiently into the phone. "You need to return that cart to the back and let *us* go up first, then you follow."

We did as we were told even though it wasn't normal procedure. Lisa fumed but complied. "He's such an idiot," she muttered. I hoped nobody could hear her.

Passengers stared at us as we pulled the cart to the back instead of serving from it. Jim and Beth took the meal cart to the front, and we followed behind them. I took a deep breath, and started serving drinks. A man at the bulkhead row had his bare feet propped on the wall. I felt like telling him to put his feet back on the floor, but didn't.

Do they do this at home too?

A family watched their child ask for a drink and receive it, without a "please" or a "thank you."

"You're WELCOME!" I said, handing over the coke. Was there a hint of sarcasm in my voice? I was feeling weary, the last days of flying were catching up to me.

Chill. You're letting stuff get to you, said a voice inside me.

Trouble began when Jim and Beth discovered that they hadn't properly stocked their meal cart. Instead of having both choices—chicken or pasta to offer, they only had chicken. Passengers knew there were two choices since I'd made an announcement. And of course, some wanted the pasta that was not available on the cart.

Now, we—the beverage girls, were in the way. Our cart blocked Jim and Beth's access to the rear galley, so they couldn't get to the pasta.

There's a reason for following procedure, fool, I thought.

I was prepared to tell Jim what I was thinking. We had to finish our service first. Then I'd tell him. Lisa made moves to pull the beverage cart back again so that they could get to the pasta and stock their cart properly.

We stopped and looked at each other.

"What would you like us to do now?" I asked Jim.

"Never mind. We'll hand out all the chicken and come back and give pasta to the ones who want it. They'll just have to wait. It's so stupid to have choices. This isn't a damn restaurant," he said.

We continued cart to cart, slowly inching to the back, serving each row, trying to be pleasant, turmoil notwithstanding. Lisa gave me a knowing glance that implied we'd proven the point that we'd been trying to make during the briefing. We served the drinks, front to back, as the other two served only chicken, leaving gaps in between where pasta was needed. In the galley, Jim took the pasta out, filling the requests of the non-chicken eaters. Beth seemed frazzled. I felt sorry that she had to work meals with Jim.

Lisa and I restocked the cart for the second beverage service. When Jim came back from the pasta duties, he barked at us both.

"I told you to set up JUST for coffee, tea or water on the second go-around."

I'd had enough.

"Listen, Jim, ever since you started reinventing the service procedure things haven't gone smoothly. In fact, this whole service has been a fiasco. Maybe you should have listened to OUR input in the briefing room—to follow procedure. This isn't working. There's a reason procedures are written a certain way. There've been studies on the best practices and your way obviously doesn't work."

I continued re-stocking the cart with all the available beverage cans.

"And I'm offering second beverages—whatever they want. Not just coffee, tea or water." Beth and Lisa watched as I confronted him.

Whoa Mary. My inner voice cautioned me. *That's enough.* No—maybe not.

"Furthermore," I continued, "you're being very controlling. Our job is a team sport, we're supposed to work together, and follow procedure. Nobody likes taking orders from anyone."

Jim left the galley to begin retrieving meal trays, and ran into another glitch. The pasta people weren't finished eating yet since they'd gotten their entrees late. The flow was disorganized, and the beverage cart was ready to go out but the meal cart was still in the way. Our service, which should have taken two hours, lasted more than three hours once we were finished. Passengers were getting impatient sitting with finished meal trays. Others waited too long for their second drink.

We were disorganized and it showed. I felt embarrassed.

One man wanted an after-dinner drink. I gave it to him free of charge.

At the end of the flight Jim apologized. I felt sorry for him. He was clueless and controlling and didn't know it. I hoped he'd learned a lesson.

We couldn't wait to land and get to our hotel.

I got to my room in Brussels, took my nap and then went to the gym on the 15th floor. Working out always helped me clear my thoughts. Later I took a long walk to the chocolate store and stocked up. That night I ordered room service. I took a long hot bath before going to bed for the eight hours I needed to get me back to the U.S. and home. *Home!*

The flight back went much more smoothly, with service procedures nicely being followed. We got along. The fact that Jim had apologized meant everything to all of us and set the stage for a successful flight back to Philly as one happy crew.

⌒

*I*t's been said that things happen in three's, and that a full moon can generate crazy phenomena. I became a believer. The last nine days proved this to be true. The three trips exhausted me, not just by the sheer endurance flying back and forth across the Atlantic, but also the human factors—passengers *and* crew.

Nevertheless, beyond any doubt, I still loved the job that produced such different experiences every time I went to work, testing me each time yet reaffirming Forrest Gump's famous line, "life is like a box of chocolates—you never know what you're going to get."

I thought about opening up the box I'd bought in Belgium, just to see.

Twenty-Nine

HIGHS AND LOWS

*I*f life is a box of chocolates, I want it all, both the bitter and the sweet. I like the ones that are hidden in wrappers as I wonder what's inside while I open them up and pop them into my mouth. What will it taste like? Crunchy or creamy? The ones that look most enticing can be disappointing while the uninviting plain pieces might surprise me with a more pleasurable taste.

I've tasted my share of the bitter and sweet, surprises and disappointments. I suspect that every human being travels through life with ups and downs. It brings to mind Forrest Gump's saying, "life is like a box of chocolates—you never know what you're going to get."

One must believe that everything we're dealt turns out for the better, barring devastating illnesses. Our paths often take unforeseen twists and turns. How we deal with the maps laid out in front of us determines whether we choose to make life sweet or permanently bitter.

I came from a family of rebellious women. My Yaya-Mary left home by eloping at a very young age. Her own daughter, my mother, the World War II bride, married my father at age sixteen. She left to live halfway across the world far from home, a loss to her family. She told me it was a scary time, leaving the comfortable cocoon in Athens. Then there was me, eloping against my mother's wishes while pursuing my dreams in the new world. And finally, my daughter Pamela. In spite of her moments of defiance, those were short-lived events that in time became sweet. Today we enjoy a great relationship.

I heard someone once say, "To be old and wise we must first be young and stupid."

My tumultuous beginning in the U.S. forced me to wake up only to realize that I had to make new choices if I truly wanted to follow my original vision to become a stewardess. It was a dream that never left my heart, a dream so strong that it fueled my intention in such a way that I pursued it relentlessly. It wasn't easy and I am thankful for the help I received from people who believed in me, starting with my parents and friends. They were the angels who encouraged my journey.

Adults spend a lot of time working; therefore our work had better be something we love or we end up as sore victims, ineffective workers and sad parents. Unhappy individuals cheat themselves and thus cheat others. And one must always find time for things outside of work that make's us happy to be alive.

There were highs and lows in my flying career, starting with the original euphoria when it began, followed with airline deregulation turmoil and pay cuts. The events of 911 made for cynical times. Bitter days in my job forced me to change my expectations or I'd be forever miserable. Those adjustments turned my lows into highs, as I trusted the airline business would improve, and it did somewhat. We had to learn to live on a tighter budget. Both John and I already knew that we didn't need a big house or lots of material things to be happy. We often spoke about the little place we'd left in Ft. Lauderdale before making our move up north to a home three times its size.

Finally, after fifteen years of living in Wilmington, Delaware we took up permanent resident in St. Augustine, Florida.

It was no easy task. First I had to convince John.

"We're spending more time in Florida than up north. Having two homes is a burden."

I'd heard a joke that went, 'There are three types of Floridians, snowbirds that flock down every winter. Butterflies that flit in and out year round (like we did). And then frogs—they croak in Florida.' I was tired of doing the butterfly thing. I want to be the frog—but not croak anytime soon.

"But I like our house up north," he argued. We fought.

"I'm tired of managing two homes, we're spending more money than we need to. I don't want to live up north anymore." I tried finding any reason I could think of.

Thankfully a bad winter with lots of snowstorms aided in convincing him it was the right thing to do. An acquaintance said, "You're not *really* going to downsize and move into that beach house, are you?"

We rid ourselves of "stuff". We had to commute again, a very small sacrifice compared to the sweetness of living in warm sunny Florida and the joy of waking up looking out the window to see lush green palm trees and tropical scenery.

I am blessed with a wonderful husband, and a sister and brother who've always been loving and honest with me. I have a few close friendships and many wonderful acquaintances.

Today my daughter Pamela is the mother that most would envy. A better mother than I ever was, she could tell you exactly the grade-point average and of what teachers are saying about her four daughters, my grandchildren—highlights of my life. She works a full time job and puts dinner on the table each night while lovingly disciplining her children to such a degree that they are complimented in public places for their good manners. They're frequent visitors of ours, and I love being the new Yaya Mary. I hope they'll remember me as I remember mine. Pamela is the wind beneath my wings now and my heart soars with pride as I witness her going through life as an adult. Do we have disagreements? You bet. But herein was another lesson for me: Letting go and relaxing into life broadened my perspectives. Keeping faith in endless possibilities instead of living in fear or sorrow is a gift that we all possess and somehow forget about. Success, after all, *is* on the other side of fear. I'd been terrified, excited, elated and everything in between. I had to let go of fearing break-ups, divorces, and interviews—and my child's sometimes dangerously adventurous spirit, before anything good could happen to me.

I see the young and the old on my planes. I often wonder what their stories are. I know they all have tales of woe and joy having tasted both bitter and sweet, and done stupid and smart things.

I am passionate about my career. What's ironic is that the things that fuel our passion can also cause mental and physical depletion. Being around people excites me. Conversely, being around so many in small spaces for very long periods of time drains me. Loud airports and endless announcements. People hurrying and scurrying. Shouting into their cell phones so that everyone hears their frantic business call or chaotic family drama. Surly TSA security checkpoint officers. Do they know how to smile? Long lines. Crowded hallways, all the things that I craved and needed, I also need less of today.

Yet I am passionate for both quiet and noisiness. I love to sing karaoke and dance. Conversely, I love quiet afternoons to read or paint.

Like others, I have to manage my inner ogre whom I've learned to summon only when absolutely necessary. But it wasn't always that way. I've had my share of altercations I'd rather forget about. Disagreements that turned into emotionally painful disputes about who's right and who's wrong. Taking a stand doesn't always mean a fight to be right unless it is a life or death situation. There were low times in my career and what I learned from those is that I have the power to manage myself under various trying circumstances.

I doubt that I could still be flying as high had I not learned these lessons.

Thirty

How Lucky We Were

*I*t was his last flight. John made a max-power takeoff. I liked those takeoffs and I knew that that was just for me.

My co-workers Susan and Melanie held my hands as we sat next to each
other on our jump seats for takeoff from Athens. My eyes welled up and
burned. Then the dam broke. I didn't try holding back the tears that came quietly streaming down my cheeks as the engines revved up to a high screaming
pitch. The galley carts and compartments shook furiously and one coffee pot
that we'd forgotten to empty before leaving, splattered all over the countertops.

Max-power takeoffs aren't the norm, and generally discouraged—they often scare the flying public as the plane shakes vehemently with the full thrust
of the two engines, and once the pilot releases the brakes it's a faster race into
the air than normal.

Pilots had to retire at a certain age. We'd been prepared for that and for this
trip. How did it come so soon? Is sixty-five really too old to fly? Nevertheless,
I knew John was ready.

Regaining my composure from the emotional departure out of Athens, I
made my bilingual announcements about movies, headsets, meals and beverages. I noticed that Melanie, Susan and Cynthia were wiping their tears off
their faces too. John was a favorite captain for many.

I avoided thinking about flying without him. We'd flown together ninety percent of the time over the last twenty-two years. We often talked about how fortunate we were.

What would it be like, flying alone again? I knew I wouldn't really be *alone*. There were other crewmembers. But it was going to be lonely.

"I don't know how you do it, fly together then live at home together," people often told us.

Our relationship was unique. We always seemed to know when to give each other space. When we needed to we leaned on each other for support. We'd share gossip and thoughts that stayed between just us. There was intimacy and lovemaking in hotel rooms in exotic places. We were comfortable flying together and very few couples in our profession got to fly together so much.

I admired his knowledge and skill in a profession coveted by many and intriguing for most. But the admiration was mutual. He respected the job of flight attendants.

"You sure know how to put up with crazy people pretty well," he'd tell me. "I don't think I'd last very long doing what you do." No he wouldn't. We each had our place—he behind the solid cockpit door at the front end of the plane, and me as hostess to the flying public in the back.

Two of his favorite co-pilots flew with us on that final trip. Dave, his first officer, had flown his first flight as a new-hire at the airline with John as his captain many years ago. Bob had flown with us several times in recent years too, and made it a point to make this trip. I was also fortunate to be working among some of my favorite flight attendants.

I'd carefully arranged a party in Athens at our favorite roof-top restaurant—a three course meal of Greek food, starting with tzadziki and bread, Greek salads, and bites of moussaka. Grilled zucchini and eggplant, French fries and an assortment of grilled lamb, chicken, pork and meatballs. The wine flowed freely. Giorgos, our favorite waiter choreographed the meal service perfectly. A three-piece band played and sang Greek folk music played on the bouzouki's, the infamous guitar-like instrument from that region. I wanted this grand finale to be the send-off John would remember. Seventeen people came, which included the flight crew, the Athens airport station personnel and a couple of good friends.

That night couldn't have been more perfect. There were clear skies, warm breezes and a full moon. Everyone who was seated at the table could see the view of the Acropolis, dramatically lit up brightly against a black starry sky in the background. It was as if the Universe had conspired for John's retirement celebration. I'd bet it did.

We were happy. But my feelings were bittersweet. I knew we'd be leaving Athens to return to Philadelphia the next day. The last flight. At the end of the party, the group split up and took cabs back to the hotel. I landed in bed exhausted, but satisfied with the night's well-executed event

The next morning John and I left our room together one last time and took the elevator downstairs. When the doors opened, our crew acted as paparazzi, taking pictures for posterity. I laughed. Really? Did we need pictures of us getting out of the elevator too? More snapshots by loving crewmembers of us on the van ride to the airport. More laughter.

"So how are you feeling, John?" First Officer Bob asked.

"I'm feeling good!" I did what I normally didn't, and held John's hand all the way to the airport. Not professional while in uniform. We all became quiet. The silence was broken when Angela said, "Last night's party was so much fun. But I had so much, and I'm exhausted!"

As we entered the plane there was a big box awaiting us. Inside it was a huge cake shaped into an airplane. It had an inscription that said, "Life is just a folly, happy retirement Captain Golly." More picture taking ensued as we sipped our coffee for some much needed pep. We decided to save the cake for later during the flight.

"It looks too pretty to cut!" someone said.

It was time to get to work. Passengers boarded the plane and I was thankful we were not full this time. John announced his welcome aboard, saying that the flight time would be ten hours and forty-five minutes. Thank God for rest breaks.

Just before leaving the gate, First Officer Dave discreetly asked me to get John out of the cockpit so that he could make his own announcement. He wanted John to be in full view of the passengers and hear it over the PA system.

"Ladies and gentlemen, this is your first officer speaking. Today is a special day for our Captain John Golly. This is his last flight as a pilot for

USAirways…" He went on to tell about John's forty-three years of flying that included the Air Force, as instructor-pilot, aircraft commander and finally airline pilot and captain.

"John, it has always been a pleasure to fly with you. You taught me a great many things, and I hope I remember the important ones at least. I will miss your guidance.

Ladies and gentlemen I hope you will join me and the entire crew in wishing John a very rewarding retirement with his wife Mary, who is also working with us on today's flight."

We could hear applause throughout the aircraft and John, embarrassed at first, waved to the passengers before taking his front left seat in the cockpit one last time.

I secured the cockpit door shut before heading to the back of the plane to my jump seat. I took one last look at John at the controls, wanting to embed that picture in my mind forever.

The plane took to the runway within minutes.

"Ladies and gentlemen we're next for takeoff, flight attendants please be seated."

The ten-plus hour flight was festive, with passengers relaying congratulatory wishes through us for John. Susan and Melanie took video on their iPads of everyone waving their goodbyes, voicing messages to John. I thought how nice it would be to play that back for him later.

He made a beautiful landing in Philadelphia.

The memories of his last flight are bittersweet. It was a gift to be able to fly together for so many years. We both knew how lucky we were.

Thirty-One

THE TRILOGY

I t was my second trip flying back-to-back Philadelphia-Athens-Philadelphia. I'd gotten used to combining my flights so that I could continue to enjoy blocks of time off.

The evening prior to this final leg, my whole crew went out to celebrate Captain Ed's birthday. We enjoyed a cornucopia of Greek food, wine, and shared jokes and laughter. The night in Athens was perfect, with clear skies and bright stars dotting the blackness. The dry air was a contrast to the humidity that was prevalent in St. Augustine. We were at a roof top restaurant—the same one where John's retirement dinner was held. Nostalgic. As I watched the sun set, I imagined it shining its warmth in America. Say hi to Florida dear Mr. Sun, I thought. Hard to imagine seven p.m. now was just noon at home. It was hot still. I felt sticky and I couldn't wait to get in the shower before turning in for bed.

Some of us took the thirty-minute walk back to the hotel while others took a cab or rode the metro. I liked the idea of working my dinner off. The walk would make me sleep better. When I got to my room I took a shower. The cool water was refreshing. I was thankful for cold air-conditioning as I snuggled under my covers and fell into a deep sleep.

When I woke up the next morning I felt good and ready for the long flight westward. It would be a full load. I was glad to have slept so well, otherwise it would've been hard flying with a heavy workload. Plenty of energy was a must.

I greeted the passengers as they boarded. Some seemed to be sad that their vacations were over. Tanned and relaxed, I suspected they'd been to the islands or on a cruise. I envied them and felt cheated by the short layovers I'd had all summer. Someday I'd go to Greece on vacation again, but not this year. I craved some down time in a whitewashed rustic hotel on one of the many beautiful islands in the Aegean. I daydreamed about the sparkling gin-clear water and fresh seafood. My reverie was interrupted when it was time to close the entry door and get ready for takeoff.

Airborne at last, we worked as a well-coordinated crew, catering to our guests with smiles. I often made small talk conversation to ask them how they'd spent their time in Greece and where they were headed.

"We're going to L.A.," one of them said, "We had a fantastic time on a sailboat with a great skipper who showed us around." That was something on my bucket list. Someday…

"So you'll be flying quite a bit before going home," I said. I couldn't imagine a ten hour flight to the states, then adding on another five to the west coast. It was almost halfway around the world.

I worked the duty free cart after the meal service with Pat. We were finishing up, heading towards the rear galley. We'd sold quite a bit, perfume and watches, but mostly cigarettes. I hated selling cigarettes. But we had to sell whatever we had available, and we'd done about $500 worth of sales that day. There was liquor, jewelry, and cosmetics. One woman alone spent $200 on cosmetics and jewelry, an inflight shopping diversion, I presumed. She was a chatty one and wanted to look at everything we had, saying it was 'retail therapy'.

Pat played it up, holding up the Grey Goose Vodka, caressing it as she walked up and down the aisles enticingly saying, "duty free, anyone?" She was fun to be with and we laughed a lot.

All of a sudden, we weren't laughing anymore.

Just as we were finishing duty free sales, I watched a woman vomit brown liquid out of her mouth in projectile mode. She'd been sound asleep and her reflux awakened her. She was startled as were the passengers seated around her. We were startled as well and rushed to stow the cart away in the galley We'd been airborne for only three hours, and still flying over land. Northwestern Europe, I imagined.

Kim who was positioned between the woman and us responded immediately. "Quick, get me some gloves," she said.

I scrambled as fast as I could to get them to her. She put them on and tended to the poor woman.

"Are you okay?" she asked, wiping the remains of the vomit off the passenger's face with towels and napkins. I doused some napkins in cold water and handed those over. I paged for a medical professional. But no one responded right away. A few minutes later I tried again and two doctors showed up, a woman and a man. They checked vitals, using the aircraft's medical kit.

Kim and I cleaned the mess on the floor, pouring Red Z on it—a coagulating substance that turns liquid into clumps for easier clean up. The rear of the aircraft looked like a disaster zone. People got up from their seats to see what was happening. There was a couple sitting next to the woman who immediately got up after she vomited. I helped them find other seats. The stench was horrible and my stomach began to lurch.

Just hold your breath, I told myself. I went to the front of the plane to find cleaner air to breathe in. When I returned to the scene again there were enough people tending to the situation, so I just stood by and watched in case they needed me.

"I hope we don't have to divert," Pat said, echoing my sentiments. But most of all we hoped the woman was going to be okay. She was travelling alone and told the doctors that she was sixty-five years old with a history of diabetes. The doctors discreetly shared that she'd also been incontinent.

"Can we help you find something else to wear? Where's your carry-on?" She pointed to the compartment above her seat.

"I didn't bring clothes. It's just a tote bag." No clothes. The poor woman. Loss of dignity and nothing to wear. What did I have in my suitcase that she could use? But nothing would have fit her. I wished I'd brought my large cotton beach cover-up skirt. That would have fit her. We gave her a blanket to wrap herself in.

It was my lunchtime, but I had no appetite. I sat on the jump seat, looked at my watch and wondered what would happen next. Would we divert?

The pilots were communicating with MedLink—the ground medical advisors for aircraft, through our two doctors. After awhile, they determined the woman would be okay. Her face regained normal color, she spoke coherently, and her vitals were good. She'd suffered from a diabetic seizure, said one of the doctors.

We gave her ginger ale and crackers, and checked up on her periodically for the remainder of the flight.

I thought she was going to die and thanked God in silent prayer that it didn't happen.

My appetite came back after an hour and I ate the lunch that had been sitting for too long—a tough piece of steak. But it satisfied me and I savored the Greek salad, not realizing how hungry I really was. Soon it would be my turn for a rest break. I was ready, after all the excitement.

Minutes later a boy who was about ten years old came to the galley—and threw up all over the floor in front of me. My shoes had specks of whatever he'd expelled from his little stomach. More unsavory smells. And now my food was asking to come up too, but I tried not to think about it. I thought I'd hurl any minute. Thankfully the feeling passed quickly. As he stood there looking helpless I was reminded of when I was his age, being helplessly airsick on flights.

I put on some gloves and washed his face.

"Are you okay?" I asked, before sending him back to his seat. Pat and I tackled the mess on the floor. More Red Z. What would we do without that stuff? I took him to his parents who were oblivious to what had just happened. They were apologetic.

I washed my hands then sat in my jump seat next to Pat who was reading a book. She paused to look up for a minute and said, "Things happen in three's."

"Oh no—let's not put that out there!" I said, hoping that we'd had the peak of excitement for this flight. We didn't need anymore chaos.

When it was time for my rest break I sat behind the gray curtains in my crew rest seat, put in my ear plugs to block noises and fell asleep. Kim woke me up a couple of hours later when it was time to do the arrival service.

"How're things going?" I asked.

"Fine. The woman is doing well, but the pilots called for paramedics to meet her. She has a connection to make in Philly, so she's not happy about that."

"Better to be safe than sorry." I said.

We went out into the aisles with beverages and sandwiches.

"How much time do we have left?" a passenger asked.

"A little over and hour."

Most everyone was asleep. It was almost four p.m. eastern standard time so it was eleven p.m. in Greece. Daylight was still shining brightly through the aircraft windows as we followed the sun heading westward.

"Would you like something to drink?" I asked my customers as I wheeled the bar cart.

"Coffee." That was the drink of choice for trying to stay awake at this stage of the flight. I felt like having one too. Maybe later.

I looked forward to going home. I'd been gone six days and even with some good rest, I felt tired and ready to be on the ground heading home.

The coffee pot on my cart was emptied quickly. I asked Pat to replenish it for me as she was closest to the galley. A few minutes later I heard her make a P.A. announcement.

"Ladies and gentlemen, whoever smoked in the rear lavatory—if we find out who you are you will be met by the police in Philadelphia. This is a safety issue and a federal violation. Smoking on the airplane is dangerous to you and your fellow passengers."

Oh my God.

Pat came back with my coffee pot filled and a panicked expression on her face.

"I smelled cigarette smoke in the lav on our side of the aircraft," she said. She said she checked the waste bin and couldn't find a cigarette butt, but doused it with water nevertheless. Just in case. Someone might have disposed of their cigarette and it could still be lit. A dangerous fire hazard.

I looked around at passengers staring at us, mesmerized. What could I say? I smiled and shrugged my shoulders. We'd be landing soon.

When we cleaned up and prepared for landing, we sat in our jump seats and stared at each other wearily then burst out laughing. A beautiful night out and friendly co-workers made everything seem worthwhile.

"See? I told you things happen in threes!" said Pat.

Thirty-Two

THE AEGEAN ON PER DIEM

t was the beginning of fall 2013. I was melancholy each time the summer season ended. I was never ready for winter coldness. Even though we lived in Florida, I'd have my share of travelling through cold and snow.

September marked the discontinuation of Athens flights since USAirways only flew the route seasonally. I eagerly anticipated May coming around so I could resume Athens flying again. It had become my favorite destination.

At the end of the season our layovers were scheduled for two days instead of one. On those two-day stays, one could relax and plan to do things one couldn't during the shorter layovers. In late September, the weather was perfect. Cooler breezes replaced the stifling heat that prevailed in July and August.

"There's something about the air and the feeling here—periwinkle blue skies and the smell of eucalyptus and wild rosemary bushes. Greece is special…it's like being in love," I said to John.

We were sitting at a small tavern in Plaka, enjoying ouzo and an appetizer consisting of tiro-kafteri, a soft cheese blended with spices. A bit later we'd go to our favorite restaurant, where my crew would join us. We called those events 'layover banquets', a frequent perk.

John came along with me on that trip. I knew he missed the layovers since retiring. He'd told me he missed the flying part—minus the simulator check rides, flight physicals and annual classroom work that was a requirement to keep an FAA pilot license current.

We were excited about this trip. As a passenger, things would be different for John. We pampered him in Business Class. The pilots were happy to see him and were jealous of his newfound life of leisure. They asked a lot of questions of him.

"So are you collecting social security now?"

"When does Medicare kick in?"

"What's the process for signing up?"

John suddenly found himself in a place of mentorship.

"What do you do to stay busy?" John rolled his eyes at me. That question came up frequently and it amazed both of us. We led busy lives. Tennis, vacations, cruising and travel—not to mention great friendships in our small town.

"I'm still trying to figure out when I ever had time to work," he replied.

Our plans were to stay in Athens the first day, walk around Plaka, the old town, and eat at the same restaurant that hosted his retirement dinner, Kritikou. Then the following morning we'd sail to a Greek island for the day. We chose Aegina because it was the closest to Athens.

Our evening at the restaurant was fantastic with food and wine flowing freely. The crew laughed and shared stories. It was the last Athens trip for most of us and I think we all drank too much wine. Nevertheless I suggested that we end the evening by going to the rooftop at the Grande Bretagne hotel for a nightcap to enjoy the breathtaking view of the Acropolis lit up at night. This was and always will be a special place for me, where my parents met and fell in love so many years earlier. We took photos of the sights from the rooftop.

"Take me home, I think I'm drunk," I said after awhile. I was tired too. More laughter and everyone agreed it was time to leave. John and I staggered to a taxi stand after realizing the metro was shut down after midnight. We weren't in the mood to walk back to the hotel. *Was it really that late?*

"Wherrre arrr you frommm?" asked the driver with a heavy accent.

"We live in the United States—Florida," I said to him in Greek

"Florida? Ah—beautiful place I've been told."

191

Home seemed so far away. I didn't feel much like chatting. The evening lights were a blur as we whizzed through traffic the way taxi drivers liked to do. It always felt like a roller coaster ride. But I was sure that the wine I drank had contributed to my light-headedness.

We went to bed immediately and I fell into a deep slumber. The next morning I woke up feeling refreshed and ready for the island adventure. I showered and lathered on some heavy sunscreen since the sun was shining brightly as usual and I didn't want to burn. We both got dressed while sipping our morning coffee.

"Let's not hurry. We don't have to go so early," John said, as I stood by the door ready to go. I was usually the one pushing to leave earlier than necessary to go anywhere. *I'm not going to be pushy today—it's his getaway too, not just mine. He's come all this way on a long flight.*

But we waited too long. I started to feel anxious. It soon became evident that John was confused about the time zone difference.

"It's nine. Our boat leaves at ten and we still have to take two metros to Piraeus and get our ferry tickets," I said. His eyes opened like round saucers, when he realized he'd calculated wrong.

"See what two months in retirement can do?" I teased him, laughing as we power-walked to the metro station. We made it to the boat within minutes of departure. *Whew.* My heart thumped heavily.

Aegina is one of many islands on the Saronic Gulf of the Aegean Sea. It can be seen from mainland Greece on the horizon. It's known for its pistachios. It was also the residence of Nikos Kazantzakis, a famous local writer who wrote the song, "Zorba the Greek". There were archaeological sites, but I didn't want to see any rocks and ruins. John respected my wishes just to linger about the island without slipping and falling over marble and rock paths or visiting boring pottery museums displaying glued-together treasures. I'd done that too many times as a child and young adult.

Aegina was picturesque with its seafood restaurants lining the bay front. When we pulled in, we strolled from the dock to explore the side streets. The further in we ventured, the less touristy. Storefronts consisted of pharmacies and clothing. There was an assortment of junk shops and bakeries whose aroma of fresh bread and cakes were intoxicating. Bathing suit shops had fifty percent sale signs on them. I didn't need or want to buy anything, but it was fun to look in the windows as we walked past them. The most amazingly beautiful part was a walk through the fish market, although I didn't like the smells. My mouth watered over the sea bass and octopus that I imagined cooked and served with olive oil, lemon and oregano. Vendors beckoned us over.

"Wouldn't it be great if we could freeze these and take them back home?"

"The U.S. customs Beagle dog would nail us," John said laughing. Ah yes, the cute little doggie in Philly that went from bags to suitcases sniffing for contraband. No meats, poultry or fruits allowed.

We went back to the street that paralleled the seaside. It was close to lunchtime, but we weren't ready to pick a restaurant. We'd brought bathing suits and I suggested we pick some place closest to the water for lunch so we could also swim.

"Let's have an ouzo first at one of the cafés. Then we can decide where we want to have lunch," John said. We walked back and forth past several cafés as we searched for the perfect one to sit in.

"How're you going to know which one?" I asked.

"Here's one—the owner lady seems friendly, she's smiling."

Perfect timing. I was ready to sit for a while.

We found a table under an awning overlooking the waterfront. It was a great place to people-watch—one of our favorite things to do together, imagining what people were up to. We'd make up stories about them.

"I wonder what he's up to," said John nodding towards a man with a fancy Mac laptop who just kept tapping away at the keyboard rarely glimpsing past the screen.

"Maybe he's writing a book," I said. A great place to do that. Especially with an ouzo and the sea air...

We ordered meatballs. I rarely drank ouzo, especially in the daytime, but it seemed like a perfect choice to do on the Greek island. The drink made me relax. The meatballs were scrumptious. Greeks make the best meatballs. They're called keftedes. I thought about my mother's keftedes and made a mental note to make some soon.

There was a group of tourists with their tour guides who sat at a separate table. They reminded me of the days I tour-guided and ate for free when I brought guests in. But after about twenty minutes the group got up and left unhappy. They were yelling at the waiter, flailing their arms and hands.

"They're from Romania. They never ordered anything to eat, but thought they had and so their food never came, because the stupid people never ordered it," said the owner, shrugging her shoulders as she walked away, shaking her head.

I could relate to her frustration since I dealt with people. But stupid?

She came back to our table. "Was I supposed to read their minds?"

We stayed a bit longer. There was free internet. I toyed with the idea of posting something on Facebook but quickly dismissed the idea as I put my phone back in my purse. It was too much fun absorbing my surroundings and being there fully present amidst everything that was going on.

After awhile it was time to leave. We strolled to the beach area but it was crowded. One of the restaurants on the water appealed to us so we settled at a table that was in the sand under a blue awning. I changed into my swimsuit under my dress. When John came out of the restroom I was already in the water swimming in the gin-clear Aegean, its saltiness lapping at my skin, cold and refreshing.

We ordered lunch. I hadn't forgotten the fish market experience so I ordered grilled octopus and sea bass with a side of boiled green vegetables. We had a Greek salad and house wine in a pitcher.

We ate slowly like people are supposed to. Living to eat, not eating to live hurriedly and by necessity. I thought about people who stood up to eat during lunch hours in the U.S. where it seemed people were driven to all work and no play. No time to sit and enjoy life's delicacies with time standing still.

We shared conversation and silence. My skin felt dry and salty from the sea. "The Aegean on per diem," I said to John. I marveled at the fact I was getting paid while enjoying this day.

A few hours later we paid the bill and left. It was almost time to take the ferry back to Athens. I looked forward to napping on the boat, but we still had time left before embarkation.

We bought two kilos of pistachios and some sweet treats from the stand alongside the small port. I found a park bench and claimed it by lying down. John sat at one end holding my feet.

"How much longer till we leave?" I asked, wondering if I had time for a quick snooze under the shady tree.

"A little less than an hour," John said.

I dozed off.

What seemed like minutes later, a "toot-toot" rang in my ears, bringing me back to consciousness. When I opened my eyes I noticed John's head slumped over, his eyes closed.

"It's time to head to our boat," I said. He woke up with a start.

"Oh no—look—it's getting ready to leave—hurry," he said.

We ran to the boat.

The captain reprimanded us for being late, albeit just two minutes. We took our seats and dozed off again.

It was a memorable day on 'per diem'.

Thirty-Three

PHILLY FACTOR

*I*t was an overcast February day at Philadelphia International Airport with dark steel-gray skies and freezing temperatures. Snow was piled high alongside the runways that had been cleared from previous days of winter storms.

I was standing at the entry door of the 767. We'd just finished boarding everyone and were ready to go. We had a light load going to Brussels that night, fewer than a hundred people. Business class was full, and I helped clear in the pre-departure champagne glassware before asking the captain if it was okay to close the airplane's forward entry door as was procedure.

"Oh wow—it's a white-out," I said, staring at the cockpit window that was accumulating snow.

"You can close the door," the captain said. "But we're going to be delayed." He made an announcement to the passengers.

"It's snowing heavily and we'll have to be de-iced," he said. "There is a line of aircraft ahead of us, so we'll have to wait our turn to be released from the gate. Thank you for your patience." We'd be lucky if it only took an hour, I thought. And that didn't count getting in line for take off.

I translated his announcement into French.

"Mesdammes et messieurs, nous vous souhaitons la bienvenue"—I welcomed them aboard before delivering the grim outlook.

De-icing became protocol on snowy days after Air Florida suffered a fatal crash in the winter of 1982. The jet's wings and a critical instrument were heavily laden with ice and snow, disabling it from effectively lifting after take off due to weight causing too much drag. It had crashed within minutes after takeoff into the icy Potomac River. There were few survivors. Ever since that fateful event, snow or sub-freezing conditions mandated departing planes to pass through a gauntlet of manned cherry pickers spraying a heated thick alcohol solution to melt the ice.

I'd looked forward to this trip. John was flying with me as a passenger again, both of us anticipating a new travel adventure. The trip had an extra long layover and we'd bought tickets for a day trip to Brugges and Ghent, towns that neither of us had ever seen.

As I walked past him now, he rolled his eyes. "I sure don't miss this part," he said.

"I bet you don't."

We'd had our share of this before he retired. Somehow these events created a domino effect where things would go from bad to worse. Flight crews affectionately called these disasters at the airport the "Philly factor."

People couldn't get to work due to the weather, baggage handlers often stopped working during heavy storms, and sometimes the de-icing machines weren't functional. Catering trucks skidded going from plane to plane on the snow-laden tarmac. Plows often couldn't keep up the job of clearing the runways. Gate agents weren't always amenable to working required extra shifts after so many delayed arrivals and departures. They had their families awaiting them at home during these inclement times.

The downside to the job I'd coveted for so long was that I no longer felt like smiling or carrying on small talk with passengers after being stuck together for endless hours in misery—a drain on my energy, no matter how positive I tried to be.

I needed to sit down, so the crew took turns taking a seat in the back of the plane.

We'd already shown the emergency briefing video hours earlier. Passengers occupied themselves by reading or playing games on their electronic gizmos. Some dozed off. Feeling weary myself, I envied them, not looking forward to the long night ahead.

Patience. Maybe we'll get clearance soon. Then we'll be on our way. Self pep talks usually worked.

Another hour had passed. Then two. The captain made announcements at regular intervals. "We're stuck because there are still several aircraft ahead of us also waiting. We're currently number twenty-eight to be sent to the de-icers."

Groans could be heard throughout the cabin.

As I looked at my watch I reminded myself that I'd been through this before. Sometimes these events were like having nightmares. Except they were for real.

Finally, the captain announced that we were going to the de-icing platform. Relief. I looked over at John and forced a smile. The flying time was anticipated to be an hour shorter than usual because of strong tail winds that would push us along. Consolation? I was too far away from bed and it was past midnight.

Outside, the ramp and runways were covered in snow. Dozens of icicles hung from the wings sparkling under the light on the tarmac. Snow coated the ground, looking like a thick crust. Baggage and catering trucks seemed to have a hard time maneuvering their way around. But the captain announced we were on our way.

Cabin lights turned on bright again, my co-workers and I checked to see that everyone had seatbelts fastened and seats upright and tray tables closed. That annoyed the people who were sleeping. We turned the lights off again and sat in our jump seats strapping ourselves in as the plane slowly taxied out.

Within a few minutes the pilot made an announcement. Bad news.

"Ladies and gentlemen our right engine has a valve that is frozen and not opening as it should. We're going to return to the gate and have a mechanic look at it. As soon as we know what the problem is, we'll pass that information along to you. We appreciate your patience."

We looked at each other.

"Can you believe this?" Karla said.

I translated the pilot's announcement again. More sighs and groans in the cabin.

We'd served water, pretzels and cookies and we hadn't even flown yet. An hour later we were told we had to switch to another plane. Passengers gathered their belongings and we proceeded to another gate.

The next plane was covered with ice and hadn't been cleaned nor catered. I found a seat next to John in the terminal waiting for the cleaners to do their job. There had to be a security check first. Then we'd be allowed onto the plane. We'd been stalled for four hours by this time.

It was still snowing.

"This is horrible," John said. I wished he hadn't come with me. It was so late. I was feeling tired. Achy. My body longed for a bed. Our time allowed to be on duty was limited to eighteen hours and we were still contractually obligated to keep going. Two more though and we could call it quits. There was only so much stamina left.

I kept looking at my watch, calculating the minutes.

Finally the security check was done and we boarded the aircraft. I watched the cleaners slowly getting the last of the trash off the airplane. They wore hoodies and earphones. The ones who weren't were talking to each other in a dialect I couldn't understand. Creole perhaps. No one seemed in a hurry. Instead there seemed to be an aloofness about them as if they'd been inconvenienced on this night.

We boarded the weary passengers who took their seats quietly. Most of them fell asleep immediately. We'd given out all the extra pillows and blankets. I felt sorry for their plight—and mine too. Instead of getting to their destination, they'd paid for a punishing evening. I was feeling frustrated for them.

"We haven't been catered," said Sue the lead flight attendant.

"They're on their way," one of the pilots said. I looked at my watch for the umpteenth time as the catering truck arrived and shoved food carts into the open galley slots. This group was jovial at least.

"How ya doin'?" one of them asked me. "You looked tired." *No kidding.*

They wore skullcaps that were covered with snowflakes. Maybe the overtime sweetened their lot.

Flight attendants and pilots don't get overtime. In fact we weren't paid for boarding or any time spent on the ground. Flight crews only get paid during aircraft movement. There was a small compensatory amount called "holding pay" that hardly seemed worth it.

We closed the door and left the gate thirty minutes before the bewitching hour that would make it illegal for us to continue being on duty. A few minutes later at the de-icing pad the pilots made the announcement that the flight couldn't proceed. Federal rules, too many hours on duty. We were to return to the gate. I felt sorry for the passengers. But I was also relieved, for I was now seeing double with my eyes burning. I was on the brink of hallucinating. My shoulders and feet ached. I reached into my purse for some aspirin.

Passengers were angry as they deplaned, yelling profanity and waving their fingers in our faces. I couldn't blame them one bit.

It was 3:00am. I took out my cell phone to find a hotel. There were none, as many other flights had also just cancelled. Munich, London and Brussels passengers all scrambled to find a place to sleep. Philly became a campsite with people grabbing blankets off the plane and finding benches or corners to lay in.

"I hate this airline!"

"Me too—I'll never fly this one again." Angry folks releasing their anger on us.

"We had nice crew though," one of them said.

"Thank you. I wish we could have done something for you…," I said.

I grabbed pillows and blankets from the plane. We'd have to sleep in the terminal too. I slept with many people that night on benches that John and I found in a corner of a gate. The lights were bright. The piped in airport muzak never stopped and TV's throughout the corridors had CNN repeating headline news, mostly about the snowstorm that was plummeting the northeast. I tried to get into a comfortable position, but the hard plastic benches were cold and hard. I put my jacket over my face to block the intrusive neon lighting. I used earplugs to try to diffuse noise. I tossed around to a sideways position. My arm quickly fell numb asleep, so I had to move again. We were just four hours away from our commute flight back to Florida and home. It showed full. But we had to give it try. I felt as if my mouth were full of grit. I went to the bathroom to take the contacts out of my bloodshot eyes and to brush my teeth. That made me feel a little better.

I felt dirty. My face begged for washing, but not here. Home. Just get me home.

Gate C22 had throngs of people standing around waiting to board the JAX flight. My heart sank as I watched them head to the jet way and onto the aircraft.

"Now boarding all passengers and all rows…" the agent announced. "Last call for passengers on flight 3211 to Jacksonville. Please board now or you will lose your seat." I hoped for two people to lose their seats and felt guilty for wishing that. But people kept running up to the gate breathlessly to catch the flight. My heart sank.

Think positive. Miracles do happen. I looked over at John who was putting on a brave face. Would he ever come out on a trip with me again?

The next announcement that came from the agent was, "Stand-by passengers John and Mary Golly". I couldn't believe my ears. He handed us two boarding passes. My heart skipped a beat. I smiled at John. I thanked the agent.

"You got lucky," he said. "No shows and misconnects—that's what saved you."

I slept on the flight and then got coffee for the hour-long car ride to St. Augustine. When we crossed over the Bridge of Lions and onto A1A I took in the sights of the boats moored alongside the Old City. The water was still and a shiny pale transparent blue that glistened with the orange reflections of the sun.

"We live here," I said, affirming our choice to leave Delaware.

Shower time. "I need a pressure washer," I said. Washing my face hadn't felt that good in a long while. We lounged that day and napped throughout, calling it "Pajama Day".

Flight crews shared their stories on Facebook about sleeping in airports and passenger anger. One flight attendant said she'd gotten slapped and the police had to come to arrest the offender.

That evening the news announced there would be another even more catastrophic snowstorm heading to Philly. I was happy to be home. Sorry for my co-workers who'd have to deal with the chaos.

Thankfully, "Philly Factors" were infrequent. Those events had a way of testing the nerves of the most emotionally mature. Those were the times I'd wanted to call it quits. But I still loved my job and managed to remind myself that my career mostly consisted of good trips and great adventures.

Thirty-Four

LIVING LA VIDA LODO

"I don't know how you do it," friends of mine said when I'd talk about my jaunts to Europe and back in three days, with some trips being back-to-back.

"How do you manage it?" asked a neighbor.

"To become a flight attendant you have to be a little crazy," said a colleague.

Perhaps I was, and still am, just a little crazy. Out of the ordinary. But my truth is, I couldn't imagine doing any other job. There were times I thought I could do better than be a flight attendant, as much as I'd wanted the career such a long time ago.

"You could be working for the United Nations as an interpreter," my mother once told me. The though disgusted me. How boring. I couldn't think of anything worse. Maybe I'd get paid more. Maybe it would be interesting, more important work depending on how you think about it.

I was lucky to learn all those languages. Just knowing those, I got to become a LODO.

LODO is an acronym that stands for "Language of Destination and Origin" and those of us who work as the in-flight announcers and interpreters are known as LODO's. We endearingly termed it "Lost Ova Da Ocean," in a Jamaican accent.

We got extra pay for our linguistic talents. But the extensive testing at the Berlitz language school so as to achieve qualification at the airline was no fun.

If we passed, we were placed on a different seniority list for bidding purposes, comprised of other LODO's.

I was number two for bidding on the Greek flight schedule. I was number three for French destinations and number three for Italian. That made bidding a schedule relatively easy except if I needed a chunk of time off or wanted to bunch trips together.

That's where my favorite LODO friend Reza came to my rescue.

"You never worry—I take care of LODO scheduling. I am the master LODO scheduler," he said. And a great master planner he was.

I liked to fly fewer trips. Reza took the ones I didn't want to fly. It was a relationship that was meant to be. When he couldn't take a trip that I wanted to get rid of—he'd find someone who would, and knew how to get in touch with the ones who'd take up my trip drops. That was Reza.

Born in Iran, Reza and his family fled the chaotic turmoil as a child when the Shah was deposed. They had to leave in the middle of the night, and moved to Athens where he grew up learning to speak Greek and French. He was a good-looking gay man who took pride in his appearance and his work. We became good friends after flying a trip together and realized how we liked the same things. We had a similar well-travelled background and a strong work ethic. Reza never had a bad thing to say about anyone. Dark skinned with exotic features, his smile was constant, revealing straight white teeth and eyes that sparkled.

Living the life of being LODO had its challenges. Some flight attendants resented the idea of a junior colleague getting trips that were the best in the system. They thought those should only be awarded to the top of the master seniority list, and most LODO's were junior with some having less that a year of flying. Never mind the fact that we possessed a skill that was necessary for foreigners who couldn't speak English, they felt that their seniority rights were being violated. Thankfully they were a small group of dissidents. Nevertheless they'd seek to make LODO's work harder than necessary.

"Mary, I need you to translate something," one of them asked me, beckoning me over to the other aisle—the one I wasn't working at that moment. We were on our way to Paris.

"Can it wait?" I asked.

"No."

I moved away from the beverage cart and maneuvered myself to the other aisle by way of walking to the forward part of the plane and through the forward galley, around to the opposite side. I wondered what it could be that couldn't wait until later, when we'd finish the service.

I reached my colleague as she waited for me at the row where a Frenchman was sitting.

"Yes?"

"Could you please explain that he owes another dollar for the beer?" she said.

I was dumbfounded.

"You called me over here for this?" I asked, incredulous. "That could have waited." Not to mention that one could universally make that communication without the assistance of a French speaker.

Shake it off, Mary. Sometimes I had to give myself a pep talk like that.

"La madame dit que vous la devez payer encore un dollar," I translated.

He gave her a dollar and I walked back to my side of the plane to resume serving beverages.

One time I was asked to make an unauthorized announcement.

"Can you tell them they can come to the rear galley if they need something?"

"No, they can ring for us to bring them what they need," I said.

Other times, if a LODO spoke up about deviating from procedures, we were put in our place.

"You're not the purser," they'd say.

It was that altercation that taught me to pick my battles after an ugly disagreement about service procedures that went awry; I'd lost my cool, staunchly defending what was company policy, and this escalated things more than necessary.

"Is there a mutiny on board today?" a passenger asked me upon landing.

"Why do you ask?" I said.

"That stewardess is asking us to write you up to the airline. We don't know why. You're doing a good job. Maybe she doesn't like you."

Infuriated, I wrote up the incident, which backfired when those who weren't privy to the event decided that I was a bad person as soon as they'd heard of a flight attendant writing up another. This would not have happened if the gentlemen hadn't alerted me of the solicitations to send complaints about me. It left me feeling wounded and exhausted, a time I've worked hard to forget.

"Don't worry, love," Reza said to me one day. "You're a good person. People don't believe you to be anything else."

After a few months passed, those of us who'd feuded finally reconciled, each admitting our faux pas—me with my anger and they for their unnecessary reactive stance.

A German speaker, Ulla, shared one of her stories as LODO on a Frankfurt bound flight:

"The captain informed us it would be a short taxi out, meaning that take-off would happen very soon after leaving the gate. We were all buckled up in our jump seats, when suddenly a woman got up and opened the overhead bin to take something out."

Ulla quickly got up to close the bin and tell the woman to buckle up and remain seated. The plane was on take-off roll as she noticed a portable child's potty and the woman's little boy seated on it, doing his business.

"There was no time to tell the captain to stop. I just walked back to my jump seat. Just when I thought I'd seen everything…"

Living la Vida LODO has its ups and downs. But mostly ups.

Thirty-Five

REFLECTIONS AT TWILIGHT

"What is the relationship between something that you do and the state of joy? You will enjoy any activity in which you are fully present, any activity that is not just a means to an end. It isn't the action you perform that you really enjoy, but the deep sense of aliveness that flows into."
Eckhart Tolle

It's that time again in October when I go to the recurrent training that I dreaded so much in the past. I've come to look at this time as a right of passage and am grateful for it. I'm fully prepared, having done my homework that consists of watching evacuation videos on nine different types of aircraft, reviewing the use of defibrillators, first aid and more. Refreshing what I already know how to do with confidence.

I've been to many places and known that I was always exactly where I was meant to be, even during moments of doubt and fear. There was always something to see, experience and learn. Some lessons weren't as much fun as others, but I wouldn't trade my life or job for anything.

I still have much to look forward to as I approach the twilight of my career. Being at the 'sunset' there'd be a few more years to go before retirement. I am thankful to enjoy good health and lots of energy to keep me flying.

There'd been times I doubted my job security and questioned my career choice. Maintaining family continuity with a schedule that was so fragmented and often unpredictable, especially during the first ten to fifteen years, was difficult. Many people cannot sustain relationships with flight attendants. They simply can't live the erratic schedules, thus making it difficult to be with them. It's an adjustment that few strong people can adapt to.

I suffered through two divorces and marital failures that many crewmembers endure as a result of spouses who couldn't align themselves with their mates' constant travels. I envy marriages that made it through turbulent times.

I've learned that to be in relationship, it's not only a fifty-fifty contract. It's a union that requires one hundred percent commitment to one another. To support each other's dreams and encourage each other's growth, doing whatever it takes to help make the other person the best version of themselves.

I am thankful I was given another chance at marriage. It finally found a soul mate who understood, one who shared my dreams and "got" the lifestyle of living out of a suitcase. Home one day and flying the next.

It's been quite a journey in a volatile industry with a job that began during the downward spiral of deregulation. After that came the reinvention of the airline business model followed by mergers and consolidations.

This one will be my last and I'm excited that my career will end on a high note. I am jealous of the younger flight crews who will reap the benefits of the high times ahead. Already there are onboard service enhancements with new tools being provided. Glassware is back in domestic first class. We've come a long way since the years of bankruptcies when flight crews had to beg catering for an extra bag of ice. We're becoming the largest airline, as we merge with American Airlines. Change is imminent. Some people embrace change while others despise it.

There are media social group where flight attendants are being vocal about a new tentative labor agreement that is being offered. It's a new world of informational technology, a vehicle to exchange points of view in a way that was only possible in crew rooms or flying together. There are always the groups that want more and those like me who see the latest as a good offer. I'm grateful of our CEO Doug Parker whose leadership steered us towards a promising future.

If you want to be a flight attendant, you must be able to handle the turbulence that also comes with flying blue calm skies. It's not a career for the meek. There will always be some tension. This is part of the ride.

It's ironic that American Airlines never offered me an interview when I sought to leave Eastern. Yet, within the next few years I'll end up wearing American wings and one more brand new uniform.

Someone asked me what I would change if I had to do my life over again? Nothing. I am glad that I was brave enough to cross the Atlantic to the New World, foregoing the finishing school. The adventures have been wondrous even with some pains to go along with the gains.

Life is always evolving. Youth is really *not* wasted on the young, contrary to the popular cliché. When we are young, we learn to walk. We fall and we get ourselves back up. There is a Japanese proverb that says, "fall down seven times—get up eight."

These days, like old times, thousands apply to become flight attendants and just a few hundred are hired. I share sorrow with acquaintances and friends who've been rejected. I encourage them to keep trying and to never give up, never forgetting my own trials in the process.

It was never a straight line to reach my goal, similar to an airliner flying from point to point, it often zig-zags and follows navigational advice from the ground—its support system.

The sweet spot is in the journey on the way towards the destination.

Many new flight attendant graduates of today are young enough to be my grandchildren. If someone had said I'd be working in my sixties I would never have believed it. I always thought I'd do it for a few years and move on. But flying is still much fun.

Fellow colleagues have written funny things about our job: It is true that we can pack for a two-week trip in one roll aboard suitcase. We know the weather forecast in countries that are miles away. Our thighs are often covered with bruises from armrests and elbows. We own stacks of pens and note pads with hotel names on them. When we hear a bell ring, automatic response is to think a passenger must be ringing for a drink. We think of cities in terms of three-letter airport codes. We are a culture unto ourselves.

hat's next? My art room awaits me. I look forward to spending more time with family and watching my grandchildren discover their passions. I will help them achieve their desires and be their cheerleader.

I want to travel for leisure using the perks that came with my job and write more stories.

Until then I shall savor my last few years of flying and being in service to others as I try to make their journey more pleasant.

I am involved with various charities that make a difference for the sick or the hungry.

ust the other day after finishing the meal service out of Athens, I caught a little girl who had brown hair and big brown eyes staring at me. She'd been doing that since take off.

"Would you like to help me serve pretzels and water?" I asked her.

"Yes!" she said.

And the journey continues.

*M*ary Bennett Golly was born in 1952. Her parents met in Athens, Greece during World War II, then settled in Sao Paolo, Brazil, Mary's birthplace. Her father was a captain in the British Army, her mother the daughter of the Chief of Police of Athens.

Her father's career with Goodyear took the family to Europe where he opened corporate offices and factories.

Mary attended elementary school in Paris, middle school in Rome and high school at the American Community School of Athens. She speaks fluent French, Italian and Greek.

In 1971 Mary immigrated to Miami, Florida and became a US citizen in 1976. She worked as a tour guide escorting foreign tourists from South Florida to Walt Disney World.

Finally realizing her lifelong dream, Mary was hired as a flight attendant with Eastern Airlines in 1984. Several bankruptcies and mergers led her from Eastern to Piedmont. The airline merged with USAirways and later with American Airlines. She still flies internationally to Greece, France, Belgium and Italy.

Mary is a Certified Life Coach, writer and an accomplished watercolor artist. She lives in Saint Augustine, Florida with her husband John a retired airline captain.

Mary's passion is to serve and to fly. She enjoys lifelong learning and doing volunteer work with various projects.

She may be contacted at MBGolly@comcast.net.